D1414657

TRIUMPHANT STRANGERS

A CONTEMPORARY LOOK AT FIRST PETER

TRIUMPHANT STRANGERS

A CONTEMPORARY LOOK AT FIRST PETER

Robert L. Hamblin

BROADMAN PRESS
Nashville, Tennessee

4213-89

ISBN: 0-8054-1389-8

Dewey Decimal Classification: 227.92

Subject Headings: BIBLE. N.T. 1 PETER

Library of Congress Catalog Card Number: 81-67206

Printed in the United States of America

To
Mary Ruth Miller Hamblin
my dear wife, wonderful friend,
and constant companion

Contents

Introduction

The purpose of this work is to give to the reader a contemporary exposition of 1 Peter. To do this required much background study. I did an exegetical study of 1 Peter in the Greek text first. Most of the translations that appear in the book are my own. Often shades of meaning have been developed from lexical studies as the result of this exegesis.

I have made certain assumptions that need to be simply stated. If this were an exegetical study these assumptions would be explained in the text; but since it is an exposition seeking to apply the message of 1 Peter to the contemporary believer, it is adequate to simply state these assumptions.

The first assumption is that 1 Peter has a secure and confirmed place in the canon. It was often quoted by early Christian writers.

Though many have found reason to deny that Peter is the author, he is named as the author in the first verse of the letter. This exposition is written on the assumption that Peter, the apostle of the Lord, was the author. Lengthy discussions of authorship appear in almost every exegetical commentary, if the reader is interested in pursuing this.

The date of authorship is a significant matter in the interpretation of 1 Peter. It has been classified by many as "The Literature of Persecution" along with Hebrews, Revelation, and James. It is evident that 1 Peter was written during a time of persecution. Three periods of Roman persecution have been documented. They were during the reigns of Nero (AD 54-68),

Domitian (AD 81-96), and Trajan (AD 98-117). Those who reject Petrine authorship usually date the work during Trajan's reign.

Nero's reign fits the era of Peter, but Nero's persecution was basically confined to Rome. It has been suggested by many that the persecution referred to was pre-Neronian and that it did not have governmental sanction. This is probably true since Peter suggested obedience to the government in 2:17. Perhaps only the rumblings of Roman persecution could be heard, but the Christians were doubtless under local persecution. A date between AD 60 and AD 63 seems probable.

The location of the recipients of the letter is given in 1 Peter. These Christians were both Jews and Gentiles and were referred to as exiles because of their identity with Christ rather than the world.

Peter wrote to them to comfort them with the assurance of God's help in their suffering and to "preach" to them. With each assurance of God's help, Peter gave an exhortation to be followed by God's people.

Early Christians accepted the words of Peter as from the Lord. Doubtless Peter's words were often read to the young churches for generations after they were written. Then they rightfully found their way into the canon. This means that the inspired message of 1 Peter has been used by Christians since the first century to bring victory in times of stress and need.

I have been blessed by the Book of 1 Peter. It was the subject of my doctoral dissertation. I wrote on Peter's use of the participle in the Greek text. That study gave me an insatiable appetite for this wonderful letter. It has been the text for many sermons. The product of a lifetime of study and fellowship with this message is produced on the following pages. It is my hope that it will help and bless you.

1
A Message for Elect Strangers

1 Peter 1:1-2

The first two verses of 1 Peter stir the human mind through an entire course of theology. The Spirit of God vibrates almost every chord of theology in these two introductory verses. Peter laid a foundation for all that is to be said in his marvelous little epistle. He was not writing, however, as a theologian, but as one who had experienced daily communication with God in his soul. These two verses reflect the whole scene of the Christian's relation to God. They stir our minds to consider both the lofty and spiritual pinnacle of election and the human response of obedience. Peter inferred the invasion of the Father into the human heart, asserted the work of the Spirit in sanctification, and acclaimed the blood of the Son as redemptive. We move through the course of election, foreknowledge, sanctification, obedience, and complete redemption. As a compact of theology, this greeting is a marvel.

The doctrine of humanity, the doctrine of God, and the doctrine of salvation all flow forth from this introduction into the rest of the epistle, as the headspring of a brook flows from the mountainside to refresh the valleys below with its lifegiving moisture. The note of common faith that stands between Peter and his readers forms a backdrop for all that remains in the epistle. Peter was writing to suffering people who needed the intervention of God in their lives. People today can feel a kinship with these suffering saints of the first century.

A Message of Revelation

The greeting rings with prophetic sound. Just as the Old Testament prophet sounded his "thus saith the Lord," Peter spoke as one echoing the revelation of God. This means that his message is an eternal message. It was a message of comfort and hope to the elect strangers of the first century; and it is no less an empowering, Spirit-filling message for the saints of the twentieth century. The authority of God is the centerpiece of the salutation. Peter did not write in his own authority. The authority of his message is in the Godhead. He wrote in dependence upon Jesus, whose apostle he is. He also wrote to mortals who were not saved by their own virtue, but the salvation within them had been initiated by God and substantiated by his grace. The revelation to Peter and to his readers, both in the first century and now, is a God-initiated revelation.

Many have marveled greatly that a letter would come from the pen of Simon Peter. Surely we could wonder that a man with his background would write such an epistle as this. Simon was a lowly fisherman of Galilee. The religious men of his day called him "unlearned and ignorant" (Acts 4:13). No doubt he was a man of little formal training. He probably had attended synagogue school when a boy, receiving an elementary education taught by the rabbi. Doubtless he did not receive any "higher" education. Some have refused to believe that a letter of such literary beauty could have come from this "ignorant" fisherman. They have failed to recognize that it was not the Galilean fisherman who was writing, but the apostle of the Lord.

The presence of Jesus in Peter's life made the difference between success and failure. Much had transpired in the life of this man of God since he had left his nets in Galilee to be a fisher of people. The most outstanding and transforming truth that could ever enter human thought had dawned in the mind and soul of Simon: he had learned with full understanding that Jesus was the Christ. It had been a very difficult course for him, but he had learned it well. At Caesarea Philippi, Peter had confessed that Jesus was "the Christ, the Son of the living God" (Matt. 16:16). This was a tremendous confession. Jesus told Simon that he had not learned this from people but had received the revelation from God. Jesus was so pleased with Simon's spiritual acquisition of this great truth that he named him Peter, the rock.

Though Simon made such a wonderful confession, he did not really understand the full significance of the fact of Christ's messiahship until a later time. In fact, before Jesus had finished explaining at Caesarea Philippi that his messiahship would mean that it was necessary for him to go to the cross and die for the world's sin, Peter said that he would not permit Jesus to do so. Jesus rebuked him strongly, telling him that now he was not understanding the revelation of God, as he had in his confession; but he was acting only upon human understanding.

Peter made other excursions into the wilderness before he really found the abundance of life. In a fit of temper, he cut off the ear of one of the men who arrested Jesus. Peter promised Jesus, at the emotion-filled Last Supper, that he would never forsake him, even if all the rest of his followers did. As always, Jesus knew the heart of this tempestuous man and warned him that he would deny Christ three times that very night. Just before the rooster crowed the next morning, Peter denied for the third time that he had ever known the Lord in order that he might save himself.

It is easy to feel brave and secure in the shadow of the Lord. His strength is very substantial when our eyes are upon him, but we become very weak when we take our eyes off of him. In the church service or on our knees in prayer, the power of the Lord is so dominating that we know we will never deny. But when the devil enters our experience with his subtle ways, it is easy to forget the Christ. It seems very rational to think that we ought to save ourselves, but God's Word says "deny yourself."

Peter finally did deny himself, but not until Jesus was resurrected from the dead. With the dawning of the resurrection, a new light transformed Peter both inwardly and outwardly. Peter went to the tomb of Jesus with John after having heard from Mary the alarming news that the body of Jesus was gone (see John 20). Peter entered the tomb and intently studied the position of the linen clothes that had been bound around the body of Jesus. The impact of the resurrection changed his life. Christ was raised from the dead! It was evident to Peter that Jesus was not a physical Messiah, but a King who would live forever and reign in his heart.

Many today seek physical evidence of the power of God. The same evidence that Peter possessed still reveals God! Jesus was raised from the dead and lives. He is not merely a character of history, but he is the living Son of God, who plants his spiritual kingdom in the hearts of people and reigns there. Jesus said, "The kingdom of God is within you" (Luke 17:21). With the resurrection, Peter learned this most astounding truth.

Peter had always been a leader among the apostles. It was he who had walked on the water. He was at the transfiguration and in the garden in Gethsemane. After the resurrection, however, he became *the* leader of the apostles. His life was filled with the inexplicable power of God. After the resurrection, Peter had several encounters with the resurrected Lord. He confessed his unworthiness to the mystifying personality of the resurrection. He prayed with the little band of believers for ten days after the ascension of Jesus, and he was filled with the Holy Spirit at Pentecost.

There is a profound lesson to be learned from Peter. As a redeemed man, he wandered through the whole wilderness from Jesus' resurrection to Pentecost, but he finally possessed the land that God had for him. From the denials on the night of the trial of Jesus to the filling of the Holy Spirit was a long and difficult journey. However, this is a journey that is often taken by God's children. We also deny the Lord when we insult him with our sin and then we have to take the long road back into his fellowship. Peter's wilderness brought remorse, sorrow, and uselessness. Like Peter, we must acknowledge our folly to the Lord and ask forgiveness. Peter's prayers must have been expressions of real dependence upon the Lord. Finally the person of the Holy Spirit empowered his frail human life. The same Spirit empowers us when we meet him on God's terms of obedient surrender.

The power of the Holy Spirit made the man who had denied the Lord a great and powerful preacher. It is surprising that a Galilean fisherman could write 1 Peter, but it is not surprising that the Spirit-filled preacher of Pentecost did write 1 Peter. The message of 1 Peter is clearly the message of a prophet who had lately been with the Lord. Actually it is no marvel that a Spirit-filled mind like Peter's could produce this epistle, but it is a marvel that we do not have more than 1 and 2 Peter from him. The great preacher Peter walked with the Lord, so his message stirred the suffering souls of saints in the first century. It still stirs our suffering lives to dependence and gratitude when the meaning of the message penetrates our minds and hearts.

Peter introduced himself as the "apostle of Jesus Christ." Since the epistle came from one that had been with Jesus, it is a message to be heard and believed. The Galilean fisherman had no claim of personal authority, but Jesus had saved him and called him to leave his nets to fish for people. All that Peter had to say to the world was said by the authority of Jesus Christ. Peter did not speak because of his ability or because of his accomplishments, but because of the accomplishments of Jesus Christ in his heart. As a man on his own, Peter had sworn, fought, lost his temper, and used a wild imagination; but God took all of the potential in this strong personality and tamed it.

If your life is committed to the Lord for full use, he will tame the wild elements and make you useful. The authority of God needs to overwhelm all of us so that we can be useful to him.

A Message for Elect Strangers

It is natural to think that the term *exiles* refers to the Jews who were scattered over the Roman Empire. By necessity the nation of the Jews had lost its identity with the country of Palestine, so those who were in other places were called exiles. However, Peter was not addressing his letter to Jews but to Christians. Wherever the Christian lives he is a *stranger* or exile. Any person who is born from above by the Spirit and grace of God becomes a stranger to the world's way of life. People of God have always been strangers. Abraham considered himself a stranger and a pilgrim among men because of his peculiar identity with God. Jesus is described in the Bible as a stranger. He was a man who had strong heavenly ties but not even a place to lay his head upon earth. Though he lived with people and became one of us, it was always evident that the home of our wonderful Jesus was not on this earth.

Whether the redeemed person is of the dispersion of Pontius, Galatia, Cappadocia, or of the United States, Brazil, England, or elsewhere, he is still a stranger because his citizenship is in heaven. As a pilgrim, the Christian may be called upon to endure hardships. It is certain that the child of God who really lives for Jesus will suffer hardships. Jesus told his disciples that they could expect to be rejected by the world, just as he was rejected. Both the saint and the sinner must suffer sorrow, pain, and disconsolation; but for the Christian, the suffering and discontent of life is only temporary because he holds citizenship in a higher realm.

Children of God may be called upon to suffer as pilgrims

and strangers because they are out of step with the world, but they are "looking for a city which hath foundations" (Heb. 11:10).

The key to understanding Christian hope is election by God. Christians may be pilgrims or wanderers in relationship to the world, but they are chosen by God. This election is according to God's foreknowledge, through the Holy Spirit, and unto obedience. The complete harmony that God intended for the human life can be realized in these ideas. It does not matter that we are "strange" to the world when we enjoy the full blessings of God's election in our lives.

The first of the blessings is a secure salvation. Christian pilgrims are secure in their future hope, not because of their abilities but because God has made complete and adequate provisions for their salvation. The saved have not attained their distinction by any human effort, but they have been chosen "according to the foreknowledge of God the Father" (1:2). This means that God proposed before the foundation of the world to redeem lost people through Jesus Christ. When Peter called Christians *elect,* it probably did not stir up the theological controversy that has since raged over the term. He was comforting suffering people. It is now a very consoling truth to know that we are *elected* according to the foreknowledge of God. It really does not matter that the *rejection* of the world comes while we have eternal security in God's election. God brings his people to repentance and faith, and he supplies all that is needed in salvation. Paul taught that salvation is eternal because it is in Jesus (Rom. 8:28 *ff.*). It is not bad to be a stranger among people when we know that God has accepted us.

The election of God is "through the Holy Spirit." The initiation of the administration of salvation to people is done by the work of God in the Spirit. Salvation is not physically or abstractly obtained, but it is obtained by God moving into the human life in the person of his Spirit. Many people think of salvation as identification with a church or the choice of a philosophy of life, but assuredly it is more than this. It is the intervention of the one true God in a redemptive act through the ministry of the Holy Spirit in the human personality.

Preachers do not need to depend upon their cunning abilities to bring people to God through Christ. It has long been a tool of the devil to cause us to think that a person's soul is secured if he gives assent to doctrines or identifies with a church. Because of the nature of sin, redemption necessitates divine intervention. The Bible is designed to bring people to a knowledge of the way of life, but the effectual call to salvation comes by the Holy Spirit. Election is actually effected by the action of the Holy Spirit. Paul said that God predestinated people to salvation, and he called those who were predestinated (Rom. 8:28-30).

After the initial experience of salvation, the ministry of the Holy Spirit continues in the Christian life ministering to every spiritual need that presents itself. Salvation includes the redemptive use of the saved. Paul said that we are saved by grace but that God foreordained that our lives would be used in service (Eph. 2:8-10). The working of God's Spirit in the saved life brings the capacity for service to God. Everything that needs to be done by the children of God can be done through the ministry of the Holy Spirit in their lives. If we need to love, the Spirit of God can love through us, if we are willing for the Spirit of God to possess us.

The ultimate of election is obedience and the sprinkling of the blood. This is a reference to the redemptive work of Jesus. The Christian is saved by Jesus' sacrifice for him on the cross. The writer of Hebrews said that the Lord appeared once in the end of the world to put away sin, and he did this by the sacrifice of himself (Heb. 9:26). The sacrifice of Christ is complete and satisfactory for our redemption.

The Christian is saved to obey. The work of Christ is the means of our salvation, and the object of salvation is obedience to God. Obedience is not the means of salvation, but it is certainly a result. James said that one could not claim to have faith if he did not have works. He could only have a dead faith, which is a nonexistent faith (Jas. 2:17-18).

The people of Israel were redeemed. Their deliverance from Egypt was the symbol of their redemption. They were, however, disobedient so they did not possess the Promised Land for forty years. The elect stranger is elected to obedience. She may have redemption, but if she is not obedient, then she will lose the happiness, power, and victory that life can have.

Christ was a stranger among people, but he was an obedient stranger. Obedience is not easy; it was not easy for Jesus. The New Testament teaches that Jesus was continuously tempted. Luke 4:13 says that the "devil left him for a season," but we can be sure that he was always returning. In Gethsemane, the devil sought to get Jesus to be some other kind of Savior other than a suffering and dying Savior. Paul tells us that he was obedient even unto the death of the cross (Phil. 2:7-8).

Obedience to God may mean a life of suffering. If there are crosses to be borne, then we must obediently carry the load. We are strangers to the world, but elect with God. He will help us carry our burdens if we are doing it obediently.

Grace and peace come to the elect stranger as he trusts the Lord and commits his life to him. Grace is the heart of the attitude of God to people. Elect strangers have received *the* grace of God in receiving salvation, but they are always receiving the grace of God for daily communion with him and moment by moment power. As the elect stranger faces suffering or persecution, he will have the grace of God for his strength and victory.

The result of the continuous flow of grace is an inward peace for the Christian. No matter how complex life may become, if the Christian is depending upon the Lord for grace, the peace of God will fill his life. We never deserve the favor of God; but, if we wait upon the Lord, his peace will flood our hearts even in the strange circumstance of adversity. The multitudes of the world have gone down to the physical god of security to ask for peace, but they have found none there. Peace comes from the God of grace who reveals himself in Jesus.

You are in a strange world, child of God. You are a stranger. You may be suffering, but you have the greatest gift in the world: Jesus the Redeemer. Through the Son, the Father has provided salvation. Through the Spirit, he has provided a power and courage for life to make it possible for you to be used by him as pilgrims in a strange land. We are strangers but elected to redemption and service, called to that redemption, and empowered to that service by the Holy Spirit.

2
Victory Is Possible

1 Peter 1:3-12

Victory is a word that has been used in many ways. A pastor called it a victory when his church pledged three-fourths of its proposed budget. Another claimed victory when his strife-torn congregation voted to retain him as pastor. What is a victory? One can answer that only after one knows what the issue is. Soldiers must have a goal before they can claim a victory. If their goal is the unconditional surrender of the enemy, then victory is not won until unconditional surrender is absolutely obtained. If the real goal of a pastor was to pledge three-fourths of the proposed budget, or to remain as pastor of a strife-torn church, then victories were attained. If the purpose was to pledge all of the proposed budget, then victory was only partially attained. If the unity of the church was the purpose, then the retention of the pastor may or may not have been a move toward victory, but it certainly was not victory.

What is victory in the Christian life? Jesus answered that for us when he said, "Be ye perfect as I am perfect" (Matt. 5:48). Ultimate victory for the Christian life is perfection. This may seem impossible, yet it was certainly a relevant ideal or Jesus would not have given the command. Perfection is our goal, and nothing short of this is complete victory. However, we will find victorious lives as we move toward this ultimate goal. Daily victories come when we walk in fellowship with Jesus, committing all that we possess into his hands.

Even in the suffering agonies of life, victory is found in moving toward the ideals of Jesus Christ. The message of

1 Peter begins with the sound of faith ringing in every tone. Terrible things were about to happen to those who would read this epistle. Persecution from Rome was as inevitable as is the storm when the cloudy bank in the northwestern sky begins to roll forth its song of thunder. On the horizon of history stood Nero, already beginning his bitter and bloody persecution of the Christians. Peter wrote to people who could hear the distant dirge of death. He did not write to say that persecution would not come, nor did he write to say that they would not be affected by Nero's tragic blow. He wrote to say that God was to be blessed because of the gracious, hopeful life now and in eternity for all who believe on him. Regardless of how severe the persecution would be, the Christians still had the glorious hope of God glowing in their hearts. This hope of God was to be their companion of comfort.

Today the ultimate victory is realized in life by trusting the Lord, as Peter instructed these early Christians to do. Some Christians are being persecuted today. The constant temptations of the devil can be felt by all Christians. The pricks of persecution for faith are known by many. We may not be suffering now, as were the Christians in the first century, but it still takes courage to demonstrate faith in Christ. It still brings sacrifice and suffering to be committed fully to the will of God. Peter insists that people should not try to turn from this persecution, but that we should willingly bear it in joy because it is God's way for us.

Many Christians have physical suffering. In disease and death, often violent physical suffering comes to God's people. Peter said that this kind of suffering must be accepted. It is not beyond the scope of God's will for us to endure such suffering. It can bring the refinement of our faith, and we are to accept it. In doing so, with our trust in the Lord, suffering will become a sweet fellowship with God rather than a terrible physical agony.

Peter taught that there are many reasons to trust the Lord even in persecution and suffering.

The Victorious Life Is Divinely Produced

In verses 3 through 5, Peter praised God for the victorious life that is divinely produced. He said, "Blessed be the God and Father of our Lord Jesus Christ" (v. 3). He recognized that the source of all things was God. Peter could not describe God in any general way. The God that deserved blessings from Peter was the Father of Jesus Christ. Some have said that Peter never really departed from Judaism because he retained such a warm feeling toward his race. Paul made it quite clear in Galatians that this feeling sometimes drew Peter into rather precarious positions. But it is very evident that Peter was first, last, and always a Christian. The God who could go into the "valley of the shadow of death" (Ps. 28:4) with Peter was the Father of our Lord Jesus Christ. Through experience, Peter knew that the only real knowledge of God and fellowship with God came through a knowledge and fellowship with Jesus Christ. Peter had been with the disciples when Philip said to Jesus, "Shew us the Father, and it sufficeth us" (John 14:8, KJV). He had heard Jesus say, "The Father and I are one" (John 10:30). The God who had demanded the faith of Peter even during the tragic days of impending danger and persecution was the Father of our Lord Jesus Christ.

In our times as we face disaster, persecution, suffering, and trying times, we must face them in the strength of God through our Lord Jesus Christ. Our only approach to the strength of God is through the Son, Jesus. God is revealed today as the Father of Jesus. His strength is available now if we approach him through Jesus Christ.

The entire paragraph under consideration was a type of Christian Shema. The Jews had several liturgical forms which began with the word *blessed.* They were directed toward God as the source of hope. The benedictions were used in the daily services of the synagogues. Though Peter began his doxology with the same word as was used by the Jews, his doxology was different. He was praising God as the Father of the Lord Jesus. Peter's faith in God was a continuation of his fellowship with Jesus Christ which had begun in the earthly ministry of Jesus.

The reason for this blessing is expressed immediately. God has "begotten us again." The word which is translated *begotten* has brought about considerable discussion in theological circles. Since the word is only used by Peter in the New Testament, some have said that it is used because of the influence of the Greek mystery religions. It is true that the word was used in some of the mystery religions to describe the transformations that took place in the adherents of those religions, but it is also true that the word had been used in Jewish vocabularies.

The tremendous influence of Hellenism is often overlooked by students of the New Testament. Many students today believe that the New Testament is only a Jewish book and that it contains no Greek thought. Judaism of the first century was greatly influenced by Hellenism; therefore, as a Jewish book, it did contain Greek thought. However, whether we find the source of this term in the Greek religions or in the Jewish religion, the meaning for the Christian is the same. Peter, by the inspiration of the Spirit of God, was saying that all of those who have faith in the Lord have been given new lives and a new way of life. When one becomes the child of God in Jesus, changes take place in one's life, both inwardly and outwardly, that make one a new person.

People are not simply physical beings. Most people recognize that the "self" is not the flesh and blood, but it is a kind of indefinable personality. Many words have been used to describe this "self," such as the ego, soul, or spirit. There is almost a universal recognition that life is more than physical. Jesus taught that if one were to have life one must be born again. Peter said that the new birth is reason to praise God. When the self is born from above, it is possessed by God. The new birth brings us into a communicating relationship with

God. Such a relationship prepares one for entrance into heaven, but it also makes possible a fellowship with God now. The new birth equips the Christian to face the suffering and temptations of life.

The new birth which takes place in the human lives of believers is not the product of humanity; actually people do not merit this birth in any way. It is "according to the riches of his mercy." In a grammatical analysis of this passage, we must take the phrase "according to the riches of his mercy" with the participle which is translated "having begotten us again." New birth is the overflow of the mercy of God. The abundance of this mercy can only be measured in the cross of Jesus because on the cross the fullness of the mercy of God is expressed.

Being begotten again means more than to be saved for entrance into heaven; it means to be saved now. If we are begotten again according to the wealth of God's mercy, then that mercy is flowing constantly into our lives to prepare us to face everything that must be encountered in this world. The mercy of God not only takes us to heaven but also it empowers us to live in this world for the Lord. The wealth of God's mercy is our victory over sin, sorrow, and suffering.

The object or end of the working mercy of God is the "living hope" (RSV). Peter knew by experience how to describe the hope of the new birth. As long as Peter was only a Galilean fisherman, he had very little future in life. He toiled long and hard with little to show for it. This physical aspect of life was burdensome, and Judaism had grown very cold as a religion. There was little hope to be found in the religion of the Pharisees. When Jesus came into Simon Peter's life, he changed everything.

In Jesus, Peter found a man who gave him new life and a new way to live that life. He found in Jesus a living hope which could not be shattered by any physical or spiritual element of life. The death of Jesus did not extinguish the hope of Peter, nor did his own sin of denial diminish this hope. The extreme effort of the Pharisees to destroy Peter and his faith failed. The whip, the admonition of the high priest, and even the iron gates of prison could not take away his hope. Many years after the crucifixion and resurrection of Jesus, the founding of the church, and the empowering of the church with the Holy Spirit, Peter stood under the ominous clouds of persecution with other believers in Christ to say that the hope given by Jesus in the new birth is a living hope. No persecution that came could take away this hope.

These same clouds may be gathering about us, but we also share in a living hope if Christ lives in our hearts. Our lives may be destroyed, but our faith cannot be destroyed because it is a faith of living hope.

As a very young pastor, I knew a woman who had lost everything she owned. Her children had died when they were young. Her husband had died. She had lived in poverty. Her home burned, the fire taking her possessions and her memories. I went to her wondering what I would say to comfort her in what seemed to me to be a final blow. I found her witnessing to her neighbors, who had taken her in, about the wonderful comfort she had in the God of her salvation. She said that her hope in Christ could not be shaken. In that hope, she had always found victory. All of us who heard her were reminded of our victories in Christ.

The means of the new birth is expressed in the phrase "through the resurrection of Jesus Christ from the dead" (v. 3, RSV). The guarantee of the new birth or the spiritual resurrection of the Christian is the actual resurrection of Jesus. Jesus had died but was alive. The resurrection of Jesus had kindled a fire in the soul of Simon Peter. Before the resurrection, he had cursed and denied the Lord; but after he understood the truth of the resurrection, he told the Sanhedrin that he must preach Jesus even though they commanded him not to do so (Acts 4:19-20). To first-century Christians, Peter said that the resurrection of Jesus was the hope of their own spiritual birth. To twentieth-century believers his letter says that the power that raised Jesus from the dead is the power that brings life to all who trust him.

God not only gives to his children a hope that will carry them through times of suffering but he also gives an unusual inheritance. Peter described this inheritance as "incorruptible, and undefiled, and that fadeth not away, reserved in heaven for you" (v. 4, KJV). There is progression in the order of these two limits of the new birth. The living hope refers to the spiritual attitude of the person who is born of God, and the inheritance is the actual spiritual possession which will ultimately be attained in eternity.

The inheritance of the Christian is different from the inheritance of the Old Testament patriarch. His inheritance was a land to be possessed. That land was threatened by the ravages of war, the invasion of the stranger, and the destruction of pestilence. The inheritance of the Christian is a spiritual inheritance, so it is incorruptible. The word translated *incorruptible* is a military term referring to the destruction of the enemy army. A physical inheritance might be destroyed by the ravages of the enemy army, but the Christian inheritance cannot be destroyed. As Nero's soldiers rattled their swords, this truth must have been very helpful to the children of God. It is still great comfort to a believer to know that such an incorruptible inheritance is his. It cannot be taken away by "height, depth, powers, principalities or any creature" (Rom. 8:38-39).

The inheritance is also undefiled. If the inheritance had been earned by human deeds, then defilement might have been expected; but since it is all the doing of God, it is an undefiled inheritance. Every physical possession that we have in this world is temporary. It is hard for our minds to comprehend any possession that could not be defiled. God has made an inheritance for us which cannot be defiled by anything. Human denials and attitudes do not change the perfection of God's inheritance. People have defiled even the words of God by altering them with their own interpretations, but the inheritance which God has provided cannot be defiled by anything that people can say or do. The human body is defiled by sin. The Scriptures tell us, "The wages of sin is death" (Rom. 6:23, KJV). Sin defiles the human body causing it to die. Moving toward death, the human body passes through the process of defilement in suffering. God has an inheritance that is not ravaged by sin, so it is an undefiled inheritance.

The inheritance is also one that "fadeth not away" (KJV). Peter said that the inheritance which God has provided for his elect strangers is an inheritance that is not bound in any way by time. Freshly cut flowers are one of the most beautiful of all decorations, but nothing is more depressing than a drooping, sick, almost dead rose. General Douglas MacArthur said in a speech before congress after his return from the Orient at the close of his leadership in Korea, "Old soldiers never die, they just fade away." It is true that the human life does fade away. The human life for all of its budding glory, like the freshly cut rose, fades away. We lose the strength and vigor of youth.

Most of us begin to complain when the pigment of our hair ceases to function and lines begin to form in our faces. We say we are getting old. The truth of the matter is we are in the process of fading away physically. In this life as the physical fades out, the presence of God gives us an ever-fresh, invigorating spiritual youth. In eternity, there will be no limitations of time. There will never be an end to the inheritance that God gives, and there will never be any move toward an end of that inheritance. The world with its agonizing efforts may cause suffering here and now, but the Christian is ever empowered by the knowledge of a God that gives an inheritance that does not fade.

The inheritance is "reserved in heaven for you" (v. 4). God

has not only produced our inheritance but he is also guarding or watching it for us. Peter said that God has set a guard over our inheritance. It is a glorious thought to hear from God that our inheritance is reserved for us in heaven.

In producing a Christian life, God not only gave us a hope and an inheritance but he also gave us security. Peter said that we are "kept by the power of God through faith" (v. 5). To Christians who were suffering because of their faith, this was a jewel of hope. We know that salvation comes by the power of God through faith. Paul said, "For by grace are ye saved through faith" (Eph. 2:8, KJV). He was saying that we are saved by the power of God when we come into union with God through faith in him. God places his power over our souls through the gift of faith. Faith is a total commitment of self to God. It is believing that God is the Creator and Sustainer of life. It is believing that God is the way of salvation. It is also the commitment of self to God for salvation. This faith is the very condition of our salvation and righteousness.

Peter said that salvation is by the power of God through faith, and the saved are kept by that same power through faith. The activity of God is seen in the Christian experience of salvation both in its inception and through all of its operation. God does not save people to leave them alone to keep themselves saved. God saves people by *his* power; and, by *his* power, he keeps people saved through faith. God guards salvation through all of life, and this guarding takes place until full salvation is realized. So the Christian stands "ready to be revealed at the last time" (v. 5). Though suffering comes to the Christian on earth, there is something far better in the future.

The fullness of salvation stands ready to be revealed in the last time. We are moving toward victory, and the ultimate victory will come when Jesus returns. God guards us now, but his full grace will flow into the hearts of believers for complete spiritual refreshment in his final revelation of himself. Completed salvation in Christ is now ready. It is waiting only for the time that God has appointed. Christ has fully accomplished salvation for the saint, and its whole course will be completed in him at the time which God has appointed.

The victorious life is divinely produced. Through the new birth God has provided an eternal hope and inheritance for us. He has given us security in that hope and inheritance. Suffering will surely come in this life, and we will fall short of the complete victory that is desired over the elements of life. But complete victory has been won by the Lord Jesus Christ, and all that is involved in that victory will be realized at the consummation of our salvation in eternity.

The Victorious Life Is Divinely Tested

Verses 6 through 9 say that the victorious life which has been divinely produced is also divinely tested. There is reason for sincere rejoicing in the experience of total salvation. Just as the original readers of 1 Peter could rejoice even though they were suffering, we too can rejoice because we know that God has made complete salvation for us. The word translated *rejoice* is used in the Septuagint to express the idea of praise for God in his work of mercy. Peter told his readers that they were to rejoice even though they were suffering. It is a paradoxical idea to say that one is to be sorrowful and rejoicing at the same time. But Peter said, "Rejoice, though now for a little while if need be you have been put to grief in manifold trials" (v. 6).

The first-century Christians were really suffering, and their relationship to Christ did not erase the pain that was there. However, even in grief, they were joyously praising God. The pains of life may be felt by the children of God, but they can rejoice because of the mercy of God. Christians may feel the barbs of criticism and the goads of anguish and disappointment as they serve the Lord, but while they are feeling these pains, Christians can rejoice in the salvation that Christ has given.

The "little while" is compared to the eternity of God. The Christian's suffering can only be looked upon as temporal when it is compared to the majestic mercy of God revealed in eternal salvation. As God is eternal, so his blessings are eternal. Any suffering in comparison to God's blessings can be counted as only temporary suffering. Actually the joy of the saint so overshadows her suffering that any suffering must be considered only a passing thing.

In the passage under consideration, Simon Peter gave four reasons for suffering. The first of these is the proof of faith, the second is the refinement of faith, the third is for the response of love, and the fourth is for full salvation. When Peter referred to suffering as the trial or proof of faith, he was not saying that God had caused these people to suffer with the intention of trying their faith. He was not teaching that God *causes* people to suffer. He was saying that God was *using* their suffering to demonstrate the genuineness of their faith. God did not cause suffering, but he would bring rejoicing even out of suffering. God can make suffering a cause for rejoicing by demonstrating the reality of faith through the stress of suffering. The word that is translated *trial* or *proof* has been found in the papyri to mean genuine. The verse could be translated, "What is genuine in your faith may be found more precious than gold which shall perish though it is tested by means of fire" (v. 7). Gold is tested by fire to demonstrate its genuineness. Faith is tested by the fire of suffering, and it will stand if it is genuine. Gold is tested to *see* if it is genuine. Faith is tested to *show* that it is genuine.

Gold is refined when it is put to the test of the flames. Genuine gold will become more beautiful and durable because of the fire. Faith is more precious than gold. When genuine faith is put in the flames of suffering, it does not perish but is refined, demonstrating its beauty. Suffering then becomes a reason for rejoicing because faith will be more demonstrative under stress. There is a purifying element to the fires of suffering while we are living, but the ultimate of that purity will be the glory of heaven itself.

This is the reason Peter said that the trial of our faith is unto the praise, glory, and honor in the revelation of Jesus Christ. In suffering, there is a joy for the Christian in anticipating the revelation of Jesus Christ. In that revelation, there is a hope for the end of all suffering and a crowning glory. A day is coming when the discord of suffering will no longer play its sad dirge, but the joy of a perfect fellowship with God will make things right with humanity and God. The very anticipation of the fullness of God's love making itself known is enough to strike the vibrant chords of joy in the heart of Christians even as they suffer. They are waiting for a full revelation of the things that now can only be known in part. To anticipate the fullness of God's love, mercy, and grace at the revelation of Christ causes joy now.

While we are suffering for a little while, we are exercising love toward God though we cannot see him. Peter was not saying that his first readers had never seen Jesus with their eyes, but he was saying that in the fire of suffering they were not seeing him with their eyes. Still there was an abiding love for him. People cannot now see Jesus with their eyes, but through their faith, even in suffering, they can love him. There is a great climactic experience coming in the future when Jesus returns, but even now there is reason to rejoice in love for Jesus. In him there is rejoicing with a *joy unspeakable and full of glory*. The present rejoicing is one that defies description; the future glory is to be even greater.

To say that the joy is unspeakable or indescribable is not just an emotional expression. Actually the spiritual impact of Christ upon the life of people brings a joy that is beyond description. This joy is present even in the time of suffering. It is a joy that is filled with the glory of God. Human eyes are not seeing Jesus now, but human faith finds him and casts a fixed look upon him. Peter was not saying that back in the past people believed on Christ and now in their suffering will seek to call back that faith. Peter said that in the time of suffering, Christians can rejoice because they are *always* believing in Christ. It may be that they believed during easy times and will keep on believing during times of suffering, so Christians do rejoice even in suffering.

Again Peter called for the future hope of a full salvation as a reason for present rejoicing. Though Christianity is a way of life for the present, it is also a life with a future hope. All that is of joy in the present is merely a part of the fullness which will be known. There is a sense in which salvation has already come to us, but the future will bring the fullness of salvation. In the hour of suffering, we can rejoice in the promise of that full salvation.

The Victorious Life Is a Life of Fellowship

Verses 10 through 12 teach that the victorious life is a life of divine fellowship. The salvation that is so encouraging to pilgrims upon the earth has been revealed by God through the ages. Peter said, "The prophets . . . searched diligently concerning the time or the quality of time that the Spirit did signify concerning the suffering of Christ and the glories that should follow them" (vv. 10-11). The prophets listened intently to God as he spoke. Often in the Old Testament we read words like this, "The word of the Lord came unto me." God had something to say through the Spirit to his prophets, and they listened. God told them that a Messiah would come, that he would be a suffering Messiah, and that following his suffering he would be crowned with glory. This was a great truth to the prophets. They were willing to place all of their hopes of life upon this revelation. They searched diligently to find when the time would be that the Messiah should come, but they could not determine the exact time. Christ has been partially revealed to us through the prophets but finally and completely through the New Testament. Peter said the prophets found that the fulfillment of the promised Messiah would come to you. The gospel has been preached unto us by means of the Holy Spirit sent from heaven.

It is not necessary to turn to some other element of life to find comfort in the time of sorrow. It is not necessary to search out some new mysticism to carry us through trying days. We move toward the ultimate victory of a complete salvation in Christ who has been revealed unto us by the word of God and by the Holy Spirit. When we come into complete harmony with God, and have fellowship with him through a knowledge of his suffering Son as our Savior and through a commitment to that Son, we find reason for rejoicing. In Jesus, we move toward victory. As we make ourselves available to him, we have the strength that is needed to rejoice in suffering.

3
Pull Yourself Together

1 Peter 1:13-25

"Now you will find it necessary to pull yourself together. Preacher, help her to do this." These are the words that came from a physician in the family room of a hospital, as he told a woman about the death of her husband. The physician was telling her that she would find it necessary to control her emotions during the time of suffering, and he was telling the preacher to aid her in finding help.

This is exactly what Peter was saying to the Christians of the first century, "Pull yourselves together." This need still exists. Peter said, "Wherefore gird up the loins of your mind, be sober" (v. 13, KJV). This means that the suffering Christian, who has found himself to be a stranger in this world, will find it necessary to pull himself together.

Peter told readers exactly how to have victory in suffering. He said, "Set your hope perfectly upon the grace that is being brought to you at the revelation of Jesus Christ" (v. 13). The theme so prevalent in the last discussion is continued here. In chapter 2, we saw that Jesus is to come again and that all things will be completed when he comes. However, a close observation of the words of Peter in this passage reveals more. He said that the grace of God will be completed in the revelation of Jesus Christ, but it is already in process of being brought to us. God does have something better for his children than can be realized now, but he has not now forsaken us. God is in the process of revealing his grace that supplies all human needs at all times.

There is a sense in which the grace of God has been brought to us. When we trusted the Lord Jesus Christ to save us from our sin, the grace of God brought forgiveness. When Jesus saves a soul, it seems that all of the grace of God is poured out upon that soul. Jesus died for our sins on the cross, and he paid the full price of our sin debt. This is God's expression of grace. When one believes on Jesus for this forgiveness of sins, the grace of God is rich, full, and sweet.

Every day brings new needs. God is ready to supply every need that we have. Just as the grace of God lifts one from the guilt of sin and brings righteous salvation, this grace continually supplies the Christian with the righteousness of God in the everyday affairs of life. We trusted Christ in faith when we were saved, and he wants us to commit ourselves to his grace by setting our hope perfectly upon that grace. By this, God is continually with his children and is the power of life for them.

Peter said that we can set our hope perfectly upon God (v. 13). First of all Peter said we must set our hope perfectly upon God in the circumstance of "girding up the loins of [our] mind[s]." This means that one must pull oneself together. In the Bible, to gird up the loins was a symbol of preparedness. The term grew out of the custom of dress. The men wore long robes. When a man went out to walk on the streets the robe was pulled up and a belt was placed around the waist to hold the robe so that the legs would be free to walk. To prepare oneself for a journey would require girding up the loins.

We live in a time when tension abounds everywhere. Many people have ulcers, and an unprecedented number of men, women, and children take tranquilizers. In this age of tension, people are having mental and emotional problems. Often emotional problems become so disturbing that one is unable to get to the heart of the real problems of life. Peter said the mind must be moved away from the circumference of mental and emotional problems and go to the heart of these problems. The external things of life are not to be magnified, rather let us take a real look at ourselves inwardly.

Peter admonished, "Be sober." We are to trust the grace of God not only in the circumstance of girding up our loins but also in the circumstance of sobriety. The term that is used for *sobriety* is a word that means to have a temperate attitude toward all of life. Peter counseled that every aspect of our lives should be evaluated by the standards of God rather than the standards of the world. We should be sober in our approach to our own lives. In this sobriety can be seen a need for God in everything that is done. Our mental capacities are able to comprehend only a small part of the immense creation and revelation of God. Sober people see that God is able to do all things, and it is necessary to depend upon him. In the circumstance of sobriety, a person is willing to set her hope perfectly on the grace of God that is being brought to her at the revelation of Jesus Christ.

In this emotionally distraught world, believers should have settled minds with all of their hope in Christ. If our hope is set perfectly upon the grace of God that is in Jesus Christ, then certain ideals will become a part of our lives that will cause us to be pulled together. The three ideals that Peter mentioned are holiness, reverence, and love. Holiness is discussed in verses 14 through 16. Reverence is evaluated as a Christian ideal in verses 17 through 21. Love is discussed in verses 22 through 25.

Commitment to a Holy God

If we pull ourselves together in setting our hope completely in the Lord Jesus Christ, we must be holy people. The demand for holiness is not an arbitrary demand that God makes upon Christians, but it is a part of the victory of God over suffering. God is saying that when the time of suffering comes to his children, rather than fret about it, they are to keep their hope on the grace of God. In order to properly set our eyes of hope in a fixed gaze upon this grace, we must be holy people.

A vast change takes place in our lives when we come to know Jesus as Savior. Verse 14 says that there is a response of obedience. Converted people do not fashion themselves according to the former lusts which they had when they did not know the Lord. Paul said that people without Christ walked according to the course of this world, and they were obedient to the devil in attitudes. The total manner of life was lived in the lusts of the flesh, fulfilling the desires of the flesh and of the mind, and they were by nature the children of wrath (Eph. 2:1-3). People had no knowledge of the Lord and no concern about sin. Without Jesus in their hearts, people were willing to live in sin at all times.

In Christ, a change has taken place. We are no longer in ignorance but know Jesus as our Savior. A change has taken place within our hearts that demonstrates itself outwardly. We are now children of obedience rather than children of disobedience. In our disobedience, we responded to the lusts of the flesh willingly; but now in our obedience, we are not to live in those lusts.

The Lord is saying that a knowledge of Christ brings about a change in our moral attitudes. When a person's hope is set perfectly on the grace of God, he must fashion his life according to the moral principles of God and not according to the ways of the flesh.

Many people who call themselves Christians wonder why they are unable to feel the abiding presence of the Lord in their lives. It seems to them that sin has conquered them, and nothing can be done about it. Peter said that if we would pull ourselves together with our hope set upon Jesus, we must take a real look at our moral condition. We cannot go on living like persons of the world who know not the Lord and expect to be able to pull ourselves together in the time of suffering. As God's children, we must turn from the ways of sin.

People are to be holy and not walk in the lusts of the flesh. Peter said, "Be ye, yourselves, also holy like as he who called you is holy in all manner of living" (v. 15). The ideal of holiness is set out by the personality and the life of God. God is completely holy. Everything in the personality of God exemplifies and reveals a character of holiness. God revealed himself in his Son. The life of Jesus is a study in holiness. He was able to withstand the temptations of the devil, though the devil tempted him often. From the beginning of his ministry to the end, the devil was always present seeking to lead Jesus away from the victory that was to be accomplished in the cross. The Bible tells us that he was "in all points tempted like as we are" (Heb. 4:15). Though he was tempted, he never sinned. His life is the ideal of our holiness.

Verse 15 teaches that the Christian must actively participate in holiness. Verse 16 states how this can be done. There is a quotation from the Old Testament which says, "You shall be holy; for I am holy" (Lev. 20:7). God is teaching that people must commit themselves to God's holy character. People cannot attain holiness by depending upon their own strength to overcome temptation and sin. The way to obey this commandment is to invite the holy character of God into one's life to overcome the temptations of the devil and to be the victory in the time of need. Paul said, "For it is God which worketh in you both to will and to do of his good pleasure" (Phil. 2:13, KJV). The will to do right is placed within humanity by God. If the human life is committed to the Lord, God's will works in the life to cause it to do what is his good pleasure. Without God working in the life, sinful tendencies will be dominant.

Too many people in our society are not living for the Lord. It is hard to identify the Christian without asking if one is saved. This ought not to be. The Christian ought to be so

committed to the holiness of God that this holiness demonstrates itself in his life. God is saying that if we expect to pull
ourselves together by setting our hopes perfectly on the grace
that is in Jesus Christ, we must live the right kind of lives. No
one can expect to have victory over suffering, or in anything
else, unless commitment to the Lord is total. Since the Lord's
character is a character of holiness, the Christian must be
committed to that holiness.

Perhaps you are one of the people who says that you
cannot leave the ways of the world and walk in the holiness of
God. You can do it if you will let the Lord be your victory over
the ways of the world. To do this, you may have to leave some
of your present associations. You may have to decide that
some of the conduct that is now pleasurable to you is de-
grading your character and, therefore, must be put aside. The
resulting victories will compensate for any sacrifice that must
be made if you allow the Holy God to place the abundance of
life in you by depending upon him to be your total life.

Conviction About God

Another basic ideal which is necessary to find peace of
mind in the perfected hope of Christianity is proper reverence
for the Lord. Peter said that we are to pass the time of our
sojourning in fear. Peter began this letter by calling the readers
elect strangers. They were pilgrims in the world because they
had been elected or chosen by God. People who serve Christ
are sojourners in this world. It is easy to forget the importance
of total dependence upon his power.

It must be remembered that our God is a Father upon his
own terms. We are to pass the time of our sojourning in fear.
This fear is a reverence for God as Father. Peter said that we
are to respect God if we call upon him as our Father. The world
has found many terms to describe God. He has been called by
such terms as "the first cause," "the impersonal it," "divine

essence," the "unmoved mover," and even "the man upstairs." Jesus addressed God as Father. Those who are saved by Jesus become the children of God. If people respect God as the Father, they will be able to pull themselves together with their hope perfectly on God's grace.

Many people believe that the most important thing in life is to have "connections." I recently read of a police officer stopping a man to check his driver's license. He found that the driver's license was limited to corrective glasses. The man was not wearing glasses, so the police officer asked him, "Where are your glasses?"

He replied, "I have contacts."

The officer said, "I do not care whom you know, you still must wear your glasses." Of course the man was referring to contact lenses, but there are many people who are trying to get along in this life by knowing someone who can give them what they want.

God judges without respect of persons. He does not look at intellect, social ideas, race, culture, or nationality. God is not concerned with the exterior person, but he is concerned with the inward person. We will not get by God with our sins.

God judges each person according to his work. As a Father, he looks at the things that person does. We cannot imagine any father who would let his son go unnoticed through life. A father seeks to correct the errant ways of his child and to discipline him so that he will have the character of life that is needed for success. Our Heavenly Father does not let our sins go unnoticed, but he observes everything we do. As a Father, he has even numbered the hairs on our heads. Jesus said, in the Sermon on the Mount, that God notices when a sparrow falls, and we are worth much more than a sparrow. God is greatly concerned about his people. As a Father, he sees all of the activity of our lives. Let us reverence him completely as an omniscient Father.

We reverence God as a Father because he is a redeeming Father. Peter said that God does not redeem with corruptible things like silver and gold. We could not be redeemed by corruptible things because of the vain manner of life we have lived. If religion were only a social reform, perhaps people could buy instruction that would change them socially; but God redeems people from the guilt of sin. A vain way of life has been handed down from generation to generation. If God does not intervene in the lives of people, they go on in their sin. People do try to change their lives with physical things, but they always fail. People make resolutions and decide that they will quit their sins, but the resolutions soon are forgotten.

People cannot buy redemption with any corruptible thing; only God can pay the price. Peter said, in verse 19, that God redeems us with the precious blood of Christ. The word that is translated *precious* means priceless. A price tag can be put upon all physical things. People have determined what the physical worth of a human body is. Jewels are often called priceless, but they are not priceless because they can be purchased. Price tags have been put on parcels of ground, even upon whole nations. Salvation could not be purchased with anything that bears a price tag, but it could be purchased by the priceless blood of Jesus.

Since nothing else could pay the penalty of human guilt, the blood of Jesus is priceless. He was a sacrificial lamb without blemish and without spot. Every religious sacrifice that people have ever made has had its limitations, its blemishes, and its spots. The blood of Jesus is a perfect atonement for sin, and it is without spot and without blemish.

God the Father planned redemption for his children before the foundation of the world, and he has in these times revealed that salvation for our sakes. His fatherhood is extended to each individual. It is easy to feel insignificant in the great universe, but the Father has considered each person to be so significant that he planned salvation for him and her before the foundation of the world and has, in this generation, made it possible for each person to understand the revelation of that salvation.

God completed the act of redemption by giving his Son on the cross and raising him from the dead. The resurrection of Jesus demonstrated that he is Lord over all. God made this demonstration so that people's faith and hope might be in Christ.

God the Father judges sin and redeems from the guilt of sin by his Son. When we respect God on his terms, we are able to pull ourselves together. In the time of suffering, when our hope is perfectly set upon the grace of God, we are able to bear our suffering with complete composure. The Father, who judges every work without respect of person and redeems from the guilt of sin by the precious blood of Jesus, is one who can hold us in his hand no matter what tragic blows Satan and physical life cause us.

Compassion with God

The third ideal of the Christian life is love. Love will make it possible for us to pull ourselves together in a completed hope. Since our souls have been purified by the grace of God, we are instructed to love one another. Peter said there is to be "unfeigned love of the brother," and people must "love one another from the heart fervently." The reason for this love is that "we have been born again not of corruptible seed but incorruptible, through the word of God, which liveth and abideth" (vv. 22-23). Peter said that all physical things will perish as the grass, but the word of God abides forever (vv. 24-25). The salvation that has been provided by the blood of Jesus Christ is an eternal salvation because it is made possible through the Word of God. Since God has given such an eternal salvation, the saved should practice a fervent and unfeigned love.

Love is a divine characteristic. People think they know

how to love, when they have only affection. The Bible says "God is love" (1 John 4:8). Love is the only single attribute that can describe the total personality of God. Since we have become the children of God, we are to show the chief characteristic of God—love. We have been saved to an unfeigned love of our fellow Christians.

Stress cannot be put on a piece of glass; if it is, the glass will break. Many people have a brittle love. When the time of stress comes, their love is completely shattered. Unfeigned love is a love that stretches like a piece of rubber. Stress can be put upon a piece of rubber and it will stretch. The love that people have received from God is a love that has stretched out to us in our sin. Paul said, "God commendeth his love toward us, in that, while we were yet sinners, Christ died for us" (Rom. 5:8, KJV). This is the kind of love that God wants his children to have. Without this stretching, or self-giving love, Christians are not able to pull themselves together in hope in the Lord Jesus Christ.

Christian love is not simply external; it comes from the heart. Some of the manuscripts have it that people are to love from clean hearts. The hearts that have been purified by faith in Jesus are capable of love. Since the Lord, in love, has forgiven us of our sin, we ought to be able to love one another. Without the purity of heart which God gives, we are incapable of love; but we have the full capacity for love with him living in us. This love is to be a fervent love. Christian love is not just a superficial emotion, but it is a deep attitude of the soul. God is alive in us. The life we are living is the life of God within us. His life is one of love. Christ gave his life on the cross because he loves us. Peter said that we are to love one another with this fervent love that God puts in us. We are able to pull ourselves together with the love of God flowing through our lives.

The basis of such fervent love is the new birth. We have been begotten again, said Peter. We are not living the same lives that we lived without Jesus. When Jesus saved us, he not only forgave our sin but also gave us new life. We are now born from above; the Holy Spirit is living in us. This new birth did not grow out of corruptible seed, but incorruptible. This means that the new life is not physical, but spiritual. We have not created this new life for ourselves. God is the seed of that life. He made this new life possible by the death of his Son on the cross. The new life is an abiding life because it is provided by God. The written Word has revealed the life. The incarnate Word, Jesus, has accomplished the life. This Word abides forever, so the new life abides forever in us. Peter quoted from Isaiah, saying flowers and grass will fade away, but the Word of the Lord remains forever (Isa. 40:6-8).

The love that we are to have is based upon the presence of an eternal Lord in our lives, so it follows that his love is an eternal love. Many problems of life would be solved if people would love one another fervently. We often excuse ourselves for not loving others. We have social, economic, and personality problems because of this attitude. Sometimes we may have concluded that our personalities or social environments prohibit this love. This cannot be true if we know Christ. We need to make our lives available to the love of God. God is not satisfied with our excuses for not loving one another. He is not pleased with our excuses about inabilities because he is able to love through us. We must make ourselves available to him. Since we are born again by the incorruptible seed of his Word, let us allow the love of God to flow through us to one another. We are to pull ourselves together by exercising a completed love.

Hope is the ideal of victory in the Christian life. We are living in a world that will constantly try people's souls. The devil has temptations for us every day. If we are to get along in this world, we must pull ourselves together by setting our hope perfectly upon Christ. We need to quit depending upon ourselves for victory and depend upon Jesus. Be holy, respect God as Father, and love one another. These things are relevant ideals when we make ourselves completely available to the reign of Christ the Lord in our hearts.

4
Counting Spiritual Calories

1 Peter 2:1-10

Dietary laws have always been important to people. In the Old Testament, much was said about what people should eat and not eat. Moses discussed many foods that should not be consumed by the people of Israel. These foods were considered unclean and were thought detrimental to physical health. The people had no means of refrigeration nor of preservation for food, and the foods would spoil quickly. God teaches us that the human body is the temple of the Holy Spirit, and it should be cared for properly. That means we must eat right.

Much emphasis is being placed on the proper care of the human body in our times. Many of us have experienced the following advice from our physician, "You should take off a few pounds." Such advice is always bad news because it is unpleasant to take off a few pounds. Whenever the physicians advise us to lose some weight, they usually present us with a diet. Many fad diets have been practiced. Some have said that calories do not count. Others have said certain medications will take away the weight and one can continue to eat what one wants.

A physician advised me once that one kind of exercise would reduce weight: place both hands on the table and push straight back. In order to lose weight, one must not consume fattening foods. Some people have gone on crash dieting programs in which they have done without nearly all food and quickly lost weight. However, they have found that their health has been damaged by such quick weight losses. While they were depriving themselves of calories, they were also depriving themselves of necessary food elements. We can quickly conclude that the physical life must be properly maintained by good food and that there are certain foods that should not be eaten because they will cause the physical body to become unhealthy.

We have seen Simon Peter telling the Christians to whom he addressed his epistle that the Christian life is transcendent in its nature. We observed this in our studies of 1 Peter 1:3-12. We saw also that it is transcendent in its ideals in 1 Peter 1:13-25. Peter then said that the Christian life is transcendent in its potentialities (2:1-10). These potentialities, however, must be accepted and used. The elect stranger finds that victory is possible in Jesus. A Christian can pull himself together through faith, exercising hope, fear, and love. A proper spiritual diet will help the Christian face the trials of life.

Commercials invite us to look young and to be healthy by eating certain foods and drinking the proper drinks. We are attracted to these foods and these drinks in order to maintain the glow and health of youth. God invites us to take the right kind of spiritual nourishment that we might have healthy spiritual lives. This spiritual health will maintain our fellowship with him in the times of stress and sorrow, as well as in the times of happiness and joy.

Sources of Failure

There are undesirable foods for the soul that must be put away. Peter began his discussion with a negative approach. If the physical life is filled with things that are not good for it, healthy food probably will be excluded. If the spiritual life is filled with unhealthy activity, there will not be room for the things that are good and right for it. Many people have no time to serve God because they use their time serving themselves.

Peter knew that the readers of his epistle had things in

their lives that distracted them in their service to God. He knew that if these distractions kept them from fellowship with God, they would not be able to have the spiritual strength that is necessary when trials come. We are not different from the first readers of the epistle in this matter. There are many trials that come to us daily. We will be no more prepared to face these trials of the devil than were the first-century Christians if our lives are filled with undesirable activities.

The tense of the verb that is translated "laying aside" (v. 1) indicates that the act of putting away or laying aside the undesirable activity is to be done once for all. The Christian must make up his or her mind that there are some things that are entirely irrelevant to the spiritual way of life and that these things must be put aside forever. People are prone to look upon their sins as the normal actions of life. One says, "I am a human being, and sin is to be expected." Christians must remember that God is in their lives and they need to turn away from sin.

The first undesirable trait to be put away from the Christian life is *evil*. Peter said that the Christian is to put off all wickedness. This word is translated various ways in the New Testament. It is sometimes translated *malignity, ill will,* and *depravity.* In some of the apocryphal books, it is used to mean evil or trouble. The malignancy of ill will can destroy the very nature of Christ in the human heart. It is impossible for one to serve Jesus and to have wickedness that is not ashamed to break the laws of God at the same time. This attitude should be cast aside forever from the children of God.

There are many people in churches today who are respectable people, but they have no spiritual health because their personalities are permeated with the malice of ill will. God gave his laws because they are good for us. He did not give his laws in order to rule over us in an abusive way but that our lives might be good and happy.

Many people today scorn the laws of God. Such disregard for the laws of God makes spiritual health an impossibility. Some church members believe they can lie, steal, cheat in business, commit adultery, rob God of tithes and offerings, be covetous, and scorn the Lord's Day. Just as we cannot live on a diet of only starches, neither can the child of God live on a diet of sin. Some starch may not destroy my life, but any sin will destroy the spirituality that I ought to have as a child of God. Therefore, all wickedness and depravity must be put aside.

In this day many people question God's Word and its commands. God's children must accept God's Word in obedience in order to have the proper spiritual health. Just as we would scorn poison in our physical diets, so we ought to scorn wickedness which makes us unashamed to break the law of God.

The second trait that is undesirable in the Christian life is *guile.* This word means *to deceive* or *to use deceit.* The root meaning of the word is to *snare* or *trap.* Peter was telling believers that they needed to put aside all of the sins that threatened them. There are things that will snare the Christian. The writer of Hebrews advised us to "lay aside every weight, and the sin which doth so easily beset us" (12:1, KJV). These weights of life and deceitful snares of sin are the things that we must put aside. The devil makes many things look very attractive. There is no question that the devil made an attractive offer to Eve because she would not have accepted an unattractive offer. He still places snares before the lives of all Christians.

Every day the child of God walks in a field of snares, asking many times what is wrong with doing this thing or that thing. Paul said to the Corinthian Christians that if eating meat offended another Christian they should no longer eat meat. The snares in life may seem all right and attractive to us, yet they may destroy our influence and our Christian personalities. These deceitful snares need to be put aside in order to have spiritually healthy lives. To put aside these snares may require sacrifice on our parts. We need to remember that we are serving a Christ who sacrificed everything for us.

The third trait to be put aside is *evil speakings.* This word means *defamation.* Generally it is interpreted to mean that Christians should put aside any talk or conversation that will be detrimental. But it has a much deeper meaning. Certainly Christians should put aside every word from conversations that will be detrimental. But Peter said that everything should be omitted that will detract from the working of God in the lives of Christians.

Recently I heard a young man describing the beauty of a young lady. He said, "She has lovely complexion, and her hair is beautiful. However, you cannot see her complexion because it is covered with make-up, and the color of her hair is completely changed by a rinse that she uses." The beauty of this young woman was completely hidden by her cosmetics. Many Christians have the potentiality of very lovely spiritual lives, yet it is hidden because of the detractions of sin that has come into their lives. God, through Peter, instructed us to put aside every distraction that would keep us from demonstrating the personal presence of his Holy Spirit.

Soul Food

The need of the Christian for the right kind of spiritual food is expressed in verse 2. The term "newborn babes" does not necessarily mean that the Christians to whom Peter was writing were people who had just been converted. He was saying that they should desire milk as a newborn babe desires milk. It was not that they should have milk because they were newborn babes in the faith and later they would grow to some other kind of food, but that as children of God, they should always desire the spiritual milk of God's Word.

The need for spiritual food is seen in the expression "that

by it you may grow up to salvation" (2, RSV). Peter referred to salvation in its complete sense. He was not saying that the Christians had just barely started an experience of faith and if they would go on they would finally be saved. He was saying, that as one partakes of the spiritual food of God, one grows into a complete salvation of life. There is a great need for this salvation in the life of every Christian. Often people who say they are believers have little dedication and little concern for the things of the Lord.

The writer of Hebrews instructed Christians to leave the elementary things of the faith and go on to greater things, striving toward perfection. Peter said that there is always a need for us to grow up in the Lord. Salvation is full and complete. But there is a sense in which salvation is being worked out and will not be completed until the Christian arrives at perfection in glorification. The Christian is constantly growing toward complete salvation. There are many things in our present lives that are detrimental to us. We need to go beyond these things. We are being told in this passage of Scripture how we might go beyond these things.

We must take the right kind of spiritual food into our lives. Peter said that it is necessary to desire the spiritual milk which is without guile. The term *milk* is, of course, used metaphorically to refer to the divinely given nourishment that is supplied by the gospel. In the religion of the Jews, words, such as *water, wine, oil, honey,* and *milk,* were used metaphorically to refer to spiritual food. In the New Testament, the same words are used to express the nourishment that God has for his children.

The nourishing qualities of this milk is the first consideration. It is called spiritual milk, but the word translated *spiritual* actually could be rendered *logical* or *reasonable.* The milk that nourishes the soul must come from the Spirit himself. The Bible says, "Faith cometh by hearing, and hearing by the word of God" (Rom. 10:17, KJV). Through the Word of God, God is able to supply every spiritual need that people have. His Word is strong food for our souls. His written Word is given to instruct us in every form of righteousness. It is able to convict us of every sin and to show us the proper judgment in every question of life. The incarnate Word lives in our souls to guide us in all of the activities of life. The logical milk for life is the Word of God and the person revealed in the Word of God, Jesus Christ, the Lord. Spiritual nourishment is in this food. The human body will grow on the right kind of physical food. The soul will grow only on the right kind of spiritual food.

Perhaps you have wondered why you do not have the spiritual maturity you need to face the trials of life. Could it be that you have not nourished your soul on the Word of God and the Son of God? To nourish your soul on the Word of God will require searching the Scriptures diligently and believing all that they say. You must also let the living Son of God be the Lord of your life. There are many people who give assent to Jesus the Savior but make no commitment to the living Lord. If Christ lives, then he must reign in your heart. Spiritual nourishment is the sincere or logical milk: the Bible and Jesus.

This spiritual milk is sweet. This means that the nourishing milk of God's Word and God's Son has a good taste. Many people seem to think that to have the spiritual life disciplined by the abiding presence of Jesus would be an unhappy existence. Contrarily, it is a sweet experience to know that the Lord is always present. By feeding people upon spiritual milk, God puts a sweetness into life. The sweetness of God's precious promise of everlasting life is added to the sweetness of his presence to comfort our hearts and to supply every need that we have. The spiritual milk is not only nourishing food but also good tasting food.

A steady diet of this spiritual food is needed. Verse 3 expresses this idea. Peter was not saying that one can grow up with only a little taste of the graciousness of the Lord but that one ought to be continuously feeding upon the spiritual milk of God's Word.

I once knew a man who was physically very thin. He could not understand why he did not gain weight. He said that once a day he sat down and ate all that he wanted to eat, and he just could not gain weight. There are many people who occasionally read God's Word, and occasionally worship the Lord through prayer and church attendance. They cannot understand why they are not spiritually mature. We must make the sincere milk of the Word a steady diet for our souls.

The Banquet of the Church

Jesus Christ, as the chosen One of God who sacrificed himself for our sins, is the banquet of the church. Verses 4-10 teach that Jesus gives spiritual maturity to the church. Not only do individuals face trials but the church also faces trials. The same steady diet that will cause the individual to grow spiritually will cause the church to grow spiritually.

Christ is a living stone. This metaphorical term has the same significance as the words *spiritual milk*. Spiritual milk nourishes the body, and the Living Stone is a foundation for the life in faith. As a Living Stone, Christ is an elect stranger. Christ is a stranger to people, having been rejected by them. He is the elect of God and precious. People rejected him, sending him to the cross; but his death on the cross was the purpose of God for which he had come to the world. People can keep coming to him as a Living Stone, and he will continually supply the spiritual needs of life.

The church is a spiritual house because it is built on Christ. We are living stones because we are partakers of Christ. Paul said that the life he lived was not his own but the life of the Son of God in him. Because Christ is the Living Stone, we too are living stones. And, as a church, we become a spiritual house.

Peter told us that being a spiritual house means many

things. Jesus makes people holy by separating them from the guilt of sin. That means that Christians are priests. This priesthood makes it possible for Christians to approach the Father. God's child is made acceptable unto God, and God is made accessible unto us through the Lord. Christians are able to know the abiding and revealing presence of God.

This holy priesthood causes Christians to offer spiritual sacrifices unto God. It is not necessary to go to the altar and make burnt offerings or blood offerings as a holy priest; the Christian makes spiritual sacrifices. Paul said that God wants us to offer ourselves as living sacrifices. Our lives dedicated to the will of the Lord are the spiritual sacrifice that God wants. As a holy priesthood built up into a spiritual house, we ask and believe that God will live through our lives to make all that we say and do acceptable unto him.

In verses 6-8, Peter quoted from the Old Testament to tell why sacrifices are acceptable unto God through Jesus Christ. He said that Jesus Christ is the cornerstone of faith. He is the elect one of God, and he is precious because there is none like him. The word which is translated *precious* is sometimes translated *honorable*. If one believes in the honor of the Lord Jesus Christ, then one is made a holy priest. If one does not believe on the Lord, Christ becomes to one a rejected stone. If we stumble at the Word and are not persuaded by it but become disobedient, Christ does not dwell in our lives to make our sacrifices acceptable; he becomes a stone of stumbling and a rock of offense. Peter was saying that we may accept the Lord as the Chief Cornerstone of faith and of the church, or we may reject the Lord by unbelief, rejecting all that we are able to be by his presence in our lives. He has been rejected by many. "He came unto his own, and his own received him not" (John 1:11, KJV). God wishes that all might have faith in the Lord Jesus Christ and be built a spiritual house, but some have not chosen to do so.

Peter said that as a spiritual house we become an elect

race (v. 9). Just as the nation of Israel was an elect race of people in the Old Testament, so the children of God who believe on Jesus are an elect race. As God's chosen people through the Old Testament era, Israel enjoyed the presence of God and all of the blessings that his presence offered. We too enjoy the presence of God and the blessings of that presence as his children through Jesus Christ. Jesus is not just one by whom we may die, but he is one by whom we may live. As we have already seen, Christians are strangers to the world, but they are chosen by God. As the church relates to Jesus Christ by believing his word and accepting his grace, it enjoys all of the blessings of being an elect race.

We are also a royal priesthood. The priesthood which we have received is the priesthood of a king. God's people are described as royal people. We may be poor, we may be persecuted, we may be trodden under foot, but we are royal people because the King lives in our hearts. As we have fellowship with him through prayer and worship, we understand the relationship that we have with the King, and we know that we are partakers of his kingship.

As a spiritual house, we become a holy nation. God's people have his holiness in their hearts. A study of history reveals that many nations have risen and fallen through the course of time. Nations have fallen because of moral decay. People seldom learn the lessons of history. God's people become a peculiar kind of nation in their dedication to him. As they have fellowship with the Lord, they are built into a spiritual house that can be described as a holy nation. Such a nation is not rising and then falling in moral decay but continues to rise as holiness dwells in its people and moves them.

As a spiritual house, they are a people for God's own possession. Peter meant by this that God has a peculiar possession of the lives of the people that belong to him. He has come to abide in human lives and to totally possess them. The purpose in doing this is, "That he may show forth the excellencies of him who called you out of darkness into his marvelous light" (v. 9). God possesses people's lives to drive out sin and to demonstrate through them what he intends them to be. Without God, we were nothing, but now we have obtained the mercy of God through Jesus Christ. The darkness of sin is driven out when God comes in to possess our personalities.

We cannot get along in life as Christians without counting the spiritual calories. The child of God cannot do just anything and continue to grow in the Lord. God has a diet for us. God wants you to put aside the food that will deter your spiritual growth, and he wants you to feast upon the good food of his Word, making this your steady diet. God wants all of us to grow up in fellowship with him and in fellowship with one another by constantly reading his Word, believing his Word, acting upon his Word, and worshiping in fellowship with one another and with him. Then God will give us spiritual maturity.

5
Victory Through Self-Surrender

1 Peter 2:11-17

Why do I act as I do? This question has often been asked. From the very earliest times, people have been interested in their behavior. Throughout history people have sought to explain behavior in many different ways. The earliest people tried to explain human behavior by superstition. Later philosophers worked out systems to explain why people respond to stimuli as they do. In recent years we have turned to psychology for answers to human behavior. Psychology is the science which seems to predict and help to control the behavior of individuals and groups through understanding the underlying abilities and motives of people. However, people are different, and even psychology cannot always explain why people act as they do.

Much work is being done by psychologists, physicians, and salespeople today to develop a spirit of positive thinking. Some people think that one can create an image of oneself and act out that image. If this is true, one can be anything one wants to be. The positive-attitude philosophy works for many people. It is true that a salesperson can decide how much money he wants to make, and then if he believes in himself, he can become just as good a salesperson as he wants to be. This is true, however, only under certain circumstances. If he decides that he is a fifty-thousand-dollar a year salesperson, and he is given a territory in which it is impossible to make fifty-thousand-dollars a year, then he will not make that much money. The idea of positive thinking works as long as external circumstances allow it to work. This positive-thinking philosophy has failed many people in our times because it does not take into account that there is any possibility of limiting circumstances.

If all evil could be eradicated, positive thinking would be the only answer that we need for life. If we take into account the fact that there is evil in the world, then we must not only have a positive attitude but also we must have an undergirding strength that will take us through the times of stress.

Simon Peter again called the Christians sojourners and pilgrims. He said that Christians are heavenly colonists. The home of the children of God here on earth is a temporary home. They are looking for a better home in the future. A sojourner is one who is simply traveling through the land. Children of God travel through this land with its stresses and problems but have citizenship in a higher land. First Peter shows us that if we properly regard that higher citizenship, we will have the courage and strength to face the difficult days that we have here on earth.

Surely as God's sojourners and pilgrims we need to have a positive attitude as we face life. But we must also remember that our own strength is insufficient in the times of temptation and suffering. We must not think of ourselves as independent. We are absolutely dependent upon God. As long as we believe that our own strength is sufficient to carry us through the days of suffering, we will feel the hurt of failure. When we surrender our self-management and let God reign in our lives, we will rejoice in his victory over suffering. This is what Jesus meant when he said, "If any man will come after me, let him deny himself, and take up his cross, and follow me" (Matt. 16:24, KJV). Only in the full surrender of ourselves to God and to his ideals can the Spirit of God give his full strength to us. Until there is a self-emptying, there cannot be a divine filling. As sojourners and pilgrims, we can succeed in life if the great Shepherd and Bishop of our souls reigns in our hearts (see 2:25).

Let us observe closely 1 Peter 2:11-17 in order to learn more about self-surrender. There are *caustic controversies* involved in the surrender of the life to God. When life is surrendered, there is a new *challenging citizenship* for us. As the result of this self-surrender, there are *consummate crowns* for us to wear.

Caustic Controversies

Caustic controversies take place in our lives when we surrender to the reign of the Holy Spirit. The Bible has much to say about warfare against the foes of evil. There are lengthy discussions of this idea in 2 Corinthians 10:3; Ephesians 6:10-20; and 1 Timothy 1:18 *ff.* Here Simon Peter dealt with the warfare that goes on within persons. Paul discussed this idea in Romans 7. He concluded that the victory over self, sin, and flesh is through Jesus Christ our Lord. He asked, "Oh wretched man that I am! who shall deliver me from the body of this death?" And then answered himself, "I thank God through Jesus Christ our Lord" (Rom. 7:24-25, KJV). Only full surrender to the indwelling presence of Jesus Christ will solve the caustic controversies that constantly occur in Christian lives.

These caustic controversies are caused by a command. The command is, "Beloved, I beseech you as sojourners and pilgrims, to abstain from fleshly lusts" (v. 11). God desires that his children turn away from the lusts of the flesh that would destroy them. This has always been the command of God. It has been stated in other words, such as, "Be ye holy as I am holy." Jesus taught that his followers are to strive for perfection. Paul said that our bodies are the temples of the Holy Spirit, and they are not to be used for sin. The command of God is that saved people should utterly abstain from the lusts of the flesh. We know that God gives us this command, but the lusts of the flesh continue making their demands.

This results in conflict. Peter said that fleshly lusts war against the soul. He was not saying that the flesh is bad and the spirit is good and never the twain shall meet. He did not use the same words that Paul used in discussing this idea. Paul spoke of the flesh in controversy with the spirit. He used the word which is translated *soul* to describe the natural body. Peter used the term *soul* to describe the inward self or the total personality of a person. According to Peter, fleshly lusts, or the tendency to sin, war against the entire personality. God did not make us to be sinners; we were made in his image that we might have the capacity for fellowship with him. In the lusts of the flesh, we do not fellowship with God. For this reason, the lusts of the flesh war against everything that people ought to be. It is no wonder that people are unhappy in sin. When a person surrenders to the lusts of the flesh, his whole personality is turned away from the purpose of God. No one can be satisfied and happy in this condition.

God made people to be living creatures not dying creatures, yet they have chosen the way of sin which is the way of death. Until people surrender their lives to the reign of Jesus Christ through the Holy Spirit, they will have conflict because they will be surrendered to the lusts of the flesh which war against their souls. The conclusion of these inward, caustic controversies will be external controversies.

The Gentiles spoke against the Christians as evildoers in the day of Simon Peter. Christians were accused of all kinds of base and criminal behavior. They were driven to meeting secretly. Often people who did not know what went on in these meetings suspected the Christians of being lawbreakers. Apparently the Christians were not abstaining from the lusts of the flesh that war against the spirit. In order to establish peace between themselves and the Gentiles, so that the Gentiles might believe in Jesus also, Peter said the Christians had to behave as examples to the Gentiles.

The word which is translated *behavior* refers to the everyday, regular, social exchanges of life and not religious activities. Peter was saying that these everyday social relation-ships of God's children with the people of the world should exemplify the fact that Christ was reigning in their hearts. Many people today are won to Jesus by friends who have demonstrated peace in their lives. Some call it "friendship evangelism." No matter what the name, if we settle our inward conflicts and demonstrate a vivacity of God's Spirit in our lives, we will attract people to Jesus.

The end result of this exemplary conduct would be that "they may by your good works, which they shall behold, glorify God in the day of visitation" (v. 12, KJV). This reminds us of the words of Jesus in the Sermon on the Mount in which he said, "Ye are the light of the world. . . . Let your light so shine before men, that they may see your good works, and glorify your Father which is in heaven" (Matt. 5:14,16, KJV). When we settle our inward conflicts by surrendering our lives to Jesus Christ, we become examples that will cause people to glorify God.

The term that is translated *good works* is a word which unites aesthetic and moral elements. It is used to describe a righteousness that will show itself in beauty. Christian morality will result in a more complete surrender to God. Many people apparently have a superficial righteousness. They are able to have an appearance of righteousness, but down in their hearts the warfare of sin is still conquering them. Many churches today are filled with these people, and the result is that their influence is stymied. Peter was saying that the life that is surrendered to Jesus Christ will have an attractive morality that will draw people to it. The behavior of a person who is sur-rendered to Jesus is not a pretended behavior, but it is a serious and sincere piety that commands respect. Such morality will cause people, when they see it, to glorify God and not humanity. God does not command us to attract people to ourselves, but to attract them to him. In the Sermon on the

Mount, Jesus said that his followers were to be the light of the world, so that, "when men behold your good works they should glorify the Father."

The day of visitation is the day of judgment (v. 12). If one will surrender fully to the reign of Jesus, others will also be won. When judgment comes those who have been won will stand before God justified in righteousness because they have been influenced by this committed life to surrender their own lives to Jesus Christ as Savior and Lord.

Challenging Citizenship

Challenging citizenship will result in the lives of those who surrender to Jesus. The key to these verses of Scripture is found in the little phrase "for the Lord's sake" (v. 13). While the Christian is a citizen of heaven, he must not lose sight of the fact that he is a citizen of the world. Heavenly citizenship is, of course, the highest citizenship and should, therefore, have effect upon earthly citizenship. In all of the conduct of life here and now, a person should surrender completely to the Lord so that his activities will be conducted for Christ's sake.

Christians are to be subservient subjects for the Lord's sake. "Every Christian is to be subject to every ordinance of man for the Lord's sake whether to the king or to the governors sent by the king" (vv. 13-14). Peter was not instructing his readers to obey the laws of the land in defiance of the laws of God. He was instructing them to submit themselves to the secular authorities in order to influence people for the sake of the Lord.

In Peter's day, many of the laws of the land were probably in conflict with the teachings of Christ. In no sense does God want people to compromise the teaching of his Word, but in every sense he wants them to be examples to all people. There is much discussion in our times about the Christian's obligations to the law. Nothing has changed in this respect; we are to be subservient subjects, obeying the laws of our land. Because a law does not suit our social thinking does not excuse us from obedience to the law. We are not living in this world just to satisfy our own desires; we are here for the Lord's sake.

Anabaptists of the sixteenth century are often described by historians as eccentric people who sought to live to themselves, but who were outstanding citizens. It is said that, though their generation could not understand them, they were some of the most respected people of their times. They evidently believed that for the Lord's sake they should be subservient subjects to their leaders.

We must not live in pride, willing only to obey the things that please us. We must surrender self. We must not consume our lives upon our own fleshly desires. We must become subservient subjects, willing to obey every law for the Lord's sake if we are to have victory through the reigning Christ in our lives.

The relation of providence and powers is seen in the first part of verse 15. Peter said, "for so is the will of God." Peter was not saying that God has necessarily ordained the leadership of every earthly ruler, but he was saying that God can use the obedience of Christians to demonstrate his message and his faith among all the people of the world. It is the will of God for all his subjects to be submissive to the powers of authority. Providence does deal with these powers and through these powers.

In all probability the Roman emperor, who ruled over the people to whom Peter addressed his epistle, was an evil man. God was not putting his sanction upon an evil Roman emperor, nor does he mean that every king, president, or any other ruler has been placed in that position by the ordination of God. God does mean that if all of his people will be good citizens and obey the laws of the land, attracting attention to the goodness of their lives, his will can be done in the world.

If we are surrendered fully to God, it follows that we will be surrendered as subservient subjects to the providential power of God. Victory will come in this area of our lives through self-surrender.

Consummate Crowns

As a result of complete self-surrender, the saved will receive consummate crowns. Three things are involved in these crowns. First of all, the committed person is in the will of God. The most glorious crown that can be worn during Christian pilgrimage is the knowledge of being in the will of God. When surrendered completely to the Lord, not living under the rule of sin, and obeying the laws of the land, a person has the confidence of being in God's will. People of the world do not understand the importance of being in God's will, and they will often scoff at those who are concerned with the will of God.

Every Christian at some time ventures out of the will of God, and misery results. When one will save life for oneself one loses life, because one is out of the will of God. When one will deny oneself, one finds life because one is in the will of God. In the sphere of God's will all things work well, but out of the sphere of his will nothing works correctly. It is no wonder that Jesus said, "Without me ye can do nothing" (John 15:5, KJV).

The second crown is found in the words, "Ye may put to silence the ignorance of foolish men" (v. 15, KJV). Peter was saying that when a person's life is fully surrendered to God, there can be no legitimate criticism of Christianity. The Christian who lets God reign in his life through self-surrender muzzles the ignorant criticism of those who do not believe.

Many people are denying the Lord today. In the name of intelligence, people are saying that there is no God. Recently a person told me that I was foolish to be a Christian because Christianity was only a system of fables and myths. Many have turned from the truth. With the growing philosophy of dialectical materialism, there will be growing criticisms of the truth of God. This foolishness will not be silenced by our arguments and speeches. We will not silence a critical world of sin by our sermons. But the foolish denial of God and his presence in the world will be muzzled by the testimony of lives surrendered completely to Jesus Christ.

I have seen hundreds of people come to Christ because of the living testimonies of Christian lives. It has been said, "I would rather see a sermon than hear one." The Roman centurion who witnessed the crucifixion of Jesus said, "Surely this was the Son of God" (Matt. 28:54). This Roman soldier had heard Jesus' words but did not believe until he saw Jesus' death. Many people will hear our words but will not believe until they see the fruit of lives completely surrendered to Jesus Christ.

The third crown that is won by the life surrendered to Jesus is the crown of freedom. Simon Peter said that we are free (v. 16). However, we do not wear our freedom as a cloak of wickedness, rather we surrender our freedom to God, becoming his bond servants. Children of God surrender to Jesus Christ, knowing that all sin is forgiven. We know that God erases our guilt in the blood of Jesus Christ. The Truth has made us free. We willingly surrender that freedom and become bond servants of Jesus if our lives are surrendered to God.

If one holds to part of oneself, then one thinks that one's freedom becomes a license to do as one pleases. Paul said, "Shall we continue in sin that grace may abound? God forbid" (Rom. 6:1-2). The grace of God reigning in the Christian's heart gives complete freedom from the guilt of sin. This reigning grace also enslaves the Christian to the person of Jesus Christ and to the will of God. The Christian chooses to be a slave of God. This is not a burden, it is a crown. This crown can only be won and understood by one who surrenders completely to Jesus Christ.

The conclusion of the matter of victory through self-surrender is found in four commands in verse 17. God's people are to pay the courtesy due to human personality. This can only be done by one who is committed to God. The Lord says honor all people. The capability to honor all people is in proportion to the Christian's commitment to God. He is told to love fellow Christians who have also received the love of God. It is only possible for us to exercise the fullness of God's love toward one another through total surrender of our personalities to God.

The child of God is to fear God, meaning to respect God as Creator, as Father, and as Savior. God must reign over the human life upon his terms. The surrender of self is an unconditional surrender to God. The last command is a command to respect authority. God is to be respected as God, and our earthly rulers are to be respected as earthly rulers. Only in total respect for the rights and personalities of all others do we reflect full surrender to God.

Victory is ours in the area of exemplary conduct, but it is only possible in total surrender of self to God. We will not be examples if we do not turn from fleshly lusts to the reign of God in our souls. We will not be examples if we do not obey the laws to which we are subject. We cannot wear crowns unless we are totally surrendered to the personality of God.

6
Enduring Injustice

1 Peter 2:18-25

Have you ever been mistreated? What was your response to this mistreatment? It is human nature to retaliate when mistreated. If you kick the dog, he is likely to bite you. One concludes that if one is kicked one ought to bite, but this conclusion is wrong. Jesus said, "Ye have heard that it hath been said, An eye for an eye, and a tooth for a tooth: But I say unto you, That ye resist not evil: but whosoever shall smite thee on thy right cheek, turn to him the other also" (Matt. 5:38-39, KJV). This teaching of Jesus has been hard for people to understand. Some have found this instruction to be a joking matter, but Jesus was very serious when he gave his disciples the spirit of nonretaliation. Jesus actually taught his disciples that the way to win a person is not with force but by the spirit of love.

I remember, from the early years of my ministry, an experience that taught me that Jesus was serious in this instruction. A man in the town felt he had some things against me. He talked about me to his friends, and they repeated the conversation to me. Feeling that the matter was just a misunderstanding, I went to the man to see if we could come to an understanding. When confronted, the man was not willing to discuss the matter and cursed me violently. My natural response was to strike him, but by the grace of God I was able to walk away with a smile on my face.

What would I have accomplished if I had struck back? *I* would have had *self*-satisfaction that *I* had defended *myself* when *I* knew *I* was right. I confess that I wanted to accuse the man of treating me unjustly and wanted to tell him exactly what I thought about it. Instead I went to my study and prayed that God would give me the grace to overcome my wrath and would bring an understanding between this man and me.

The end of the affair came almost a year later when the man apologized and asked my forgiveness. We became friends, but we could not have done so if I had not followed the Lord's instructions. In the moment of my anger, I could have retaliated; but a moment of self-satisfaction would have been the only reward. Following the Lord's instruction brought a deep sense of the presence of God and resulted in the reward of a loving friend instead of a bitter enemy.

It is easy to forget the Lord's instruction, but the result will be the loss of spiritual power and spiritual influence. It is, therefore, vital that each Christian does what God wants done.

This passage was written for slaves. Peter, like other writers of the New Testament, did not discuss the lack of virtue or the presence of virtue in slavery, but he accepted it as a fact of life in his day. The slaves he addressed were Christian, household slaves. The household slaves may have done menial chores but many of them were men and women with great intelligence. Peter told these slaves that, if their Christian testimonies were to have meaning, they had to learn to suffer injustice, and they had to glorify God through this wrong suffering.

The people who know Jesus today are his servants, living in a world of sin. This world of sin produces suffering, sometimes unjust suffering. A world with a smitten conscience finds it necessary to strike hard at the principles and spirit of Christianity. Jesus told his disciples that they would suffer while serving him. He said that he had to suffer the death of the cross, and his disciples could not expect to go through life without suffering. From a human point of view, the cross of Christ was a great injustice, and so the disciples of

Jesus in our day can expect to suffer injustice also. If we will be living testimonies for Christ in the suffering of injustice, we must suffer as Christ did. We are not to retaliate against injustice, but we are to endure it.

The Virtue of Enduring Injustice

The virtue of enduring injustice is discussed in verses 18-20. Peter proclaimed, "Servants, be in subjection to your masters with all fear" (v. 20). Servants were to obey their masters because that was their obligation in life. There must have been circumstances under which obedience to masters was very distasteful to Christian servants, but their suffering would be for Christ.

There is no virtue in suffering for sin. Peter said, "For what glory is it, if, when you sin, and are buffeted for it, you take it patiently?" (v. 20). There was no virtue in the suffering of a slave who deserved the punishment he received. Many people today suffer because they are not willing to obey Jesus Christ. If a person retaliates against injustice with injustice, suffering can be expected. In this suffering there is no glory, and the sufferer will stand alone. The slave who deserved punishment got it. The Christian who sins against God deserves punishment, and will get it.

The Christian slave was instructed to endure subjection to the master who mistreated him. Peter said that this is to be done in "conscience toward God" (v. 19). To endure suffering wrongfully for the sake of God is a great virtue. The key to this entire matter is found in the words "for conscience toward God." Self-vindication is not the point in suffering. When Christians are called upon to endure injustice, they must remember that their basic responsibility is to God and the vindication of Jesus. God expects his children to serve him with their lives. He expects this service to be living testimonies of redemption. One cannot be a testimony of this redemption unless one has the Spirit of God showing in one's life. God has redeemed people by the blood of his Son in love. In God's love, with our conscience right in the sight of God, we are expected to be able to endure injustice.

Peter said that suffering injustice patiently is acceptable to God. There should be nothing more important to Christians than to do what is acceptable to God. Usually too much time is spent trying to do and be what people expect. I remember hearing a story about a preacher who was abused by a friend. The preacher took a strike upon one cheek and turned the other cheek. Then he administered a physical beating to his assailant, saying he had fulfilled the requirement of the New Testament. The man who told me this story seemed to think that the preacher was very brave. In the eyes of the world, he may have been a brave man; but in spirit he had disobeyed the instruction of Jesus. Which is better, to be brave in the eyes of humanity, or to do what is acceptable to God? God's way is far better than the ways of the world.

The road upon which God's children walk is a straight and narrow way. It is a way that is unpopular with the world. God's children are different: They may be known as cowards, they may be called meek and lowly, or the world may think of them as defeated little people. But the strength of God is upon those people who do what is acceptable in his sight. It is far better to be a big person with God and a little person with the world, than to be world renowned and a failure in spiritual things.

The Vision in Enduring Injustice

There is a vision in enduring injustice. Verses 21-23 teach that Christ is the example in suffering wrongfully. Peter said, "Christ also suffered for you" (v. 21). The suffering that was inflicted upon Jesus Christ was certainly wrong. When we attend the trial and crucifixion of Jesus through the Word of God, our hearts are moved with the injustice of it all. Jesus, who never sinned, was betrayed by a friend. Shades of the injustice can be seen in the manner of the betrayal of Judas. He betrayed Jesus with a kiss. Jesus was arrested and illegally tried. The trial before Annas and Caiaphas was an illegal trial because it was held before the break of day. No justice was found in the court of Pilate. Could anyone find justice in the decree that Pilate made? He stood Jesus before the people and said in essence, "I find this man not guilty, therefore, I sentence him to be crucified upon the cross" (see John 18:31-39). Certainly there has never been a trial in history in which a greater injustice was done.

The injustice of the multitudes was heaped upon Christ when he suffered for us. Yet, when he suffered wrongfully, he did not answer. Peter said that Jesus did not sin, there was no guile found in his mouth; but when he was reviled, he did not answer. He gave himself into the hands of the Father. Jesus did not retaliate when charges were brought against him. In the Spirit of the Father, he accepted the injustice that was given to him. He realized that the cross was God's assignment to him for the salvation of humanity. For conscience sake, because it was the will of God, Jesus was ready to accept this great injustice that was done to him. He did not argue nor defend himself. He simply accepted the gross injustice that he might do the will of God.

It is an important fact that Christ committed himself to the Father. He knew that the injustice of people must be endured, and he knew that he could endure that injustice if he committed himself to the One who judges righteously. Every Christian needs to be committed into the hands of the Father who judges righteously in the time of injustice.

Peter said that the suffering of Christ was done as an example (v. 21). The word that is translated *example* means 'copy-letter.' The student, who was learning to write in school, had example letters of the alphabet to be copied. He imitated those letters as perfectly as possible. Remember how perfect the copy-letters were which were set before you as a first grade pupil? At first you could not make those letters perfectly and your writing was almost illegible. Through the years, as you learned to control the muscles of your arms and hands, you copied the letters more perfectly.

Christ is our copy-letter in enduring injustice. If we will keep our eyes upon him and try to imitate his response to injustice, our lives will be what God wants them to be. When we pattern our lives after the normal human response, the life is not a legible testimony for Jesus. Perhaps at first we will find it difficult to copy the pattern that has been set by Jesus Christ; but as we continually discipline ourselves and respond in the way that Jesus responded, we will learn to more perfectly imitate his character when we suffer injustice.

The Vicarious Victory in Enduring Injustice

There is a vicarious victory in enduring injustice. Certainly there is virtue in enduring injustice, and the vision of Christ is an example. But this is not enough. The instruction of Jesus, in the Sermon on the Mount, of nonretaliation is difficult to follow. If God left people alone, that teaching could not be followed. But God has not left us alone. He has given us the victory of Jesus accomplished on the cross. Verses 24-25 say that Christ has won a complete victory for Christians in all things.

Christ bore our sins on the cross. He lived perfectly, though he was tempted in all points like all others. He took our sins to the cross and was crucified for them. This is our victory over all sin. It is our victory over the lusts of our flesh, the pride of life, and all other unrighteousness. In Christ, we died unto sin and live unto righteousness. Peter said that victory over sin, no matter what sin, is not left to the response of the human mind or body; it was won by the death of Jesus Christ upon the cross in our behalf. Christ took our guilt upon himself and willfully bore that guilt in his death. Christ is an example, but he is more than an example: He is the vicarious atonement for sins.

People are healed by Jesus' suffering. Peter, quoting from Isaiah, said, "By whose stripes you were healed" (v. 24). Though we were people going astray in our sins, Jesus healed us by his suffering. The victory over all sin has been won by Jesus. The child of God now is able to cast every sin upon Christ, and he erases the guilt, forgiving the person and placing the spirit of victory in his heart. The wounds that sin makes have been placed upon Jesus, and human souls are healed by his stripes. When we suffer injustice, we need to take that injustice to the cross of Jesus. If we physically retaliate for the injustice that we bear, we lose the battle. If we take our injustice to the cross of Jesus and let the "old self" be crucified with Jesus Christ, then sin dies, and righteousness lives in us. There are many things that I cannot do humanly, but I can do them "in the Lord Jesus Christ."

Peter was saying to Christian household slaves that they could endure the suffering of injustice in Christ because he had by his death on the cross accomplished complete victory for them over sin. Jesus, by his death on the cross, has accomplished complete victory for you and for me, so we can depend upon him as a vicarious victory even in suffering injustice.

All people like sheep have gone astray, but as God's children we are able to return to the Shepherd and Bishop of our souls. The ultimate victory over injustice is in complete commitment to Christ. Often people trust humans or things to provide for spiritual needs. Christ becomes to many people an abstract principle of religion rather than a personal being with whom they have daily communication and fellowship.

Christ is not a set of rules to be kept nor a system of doctrine, he is a person who wants to tend to souls like a shepherd tends to his flock. The shepherd goes in and out of the sheepfold with his flock. He sees that his flock is properly fed in the pastures and watered in the streams. He protects his flock from strangers and animals who would devour it. He even sleeps in the door of the sheepfold so that no enemy can creep in unaware and harm the flock.

Jesus tends our souls. There is no nourishment that our souls need that Jesus cannot supply. There is no cooling drink of refreshment that our souls will ever need that cannot be found in the still water that Jesus provides. There is no harm that could ever come to our souls because Jesus is at the door to keep us from harm. The world may cause us to suffer injustice, but Jesus makes that injustice endurable because he is the Shepherd who tends to every need that the soul has.

The slaves to whom Peter addressed these words were instructed not to go astray like sheep, but to stay close to their Shepherd. We must not wander from Jesus but stay near him who is our Shepherd. We can go astray, even though we are God's children. When we stray, we do not have the protection and endurance to bear injustice. Let us not walk alone through life, but let us walk with our souls tended by the good Shepherd, Jesus Christ.

Jesus is also the Bishop of our souls. The word *bishop* means overseer. This perhaps has reference to the lordship of Jesus. The vicarious victory he has won for us over sin and injustice is a complete victory. We realize that we have complete victory over guilt when we receive Jesus as our Savior through faith. We realize that this is a complete victory over sin and its reign in our lives when we accept the lordship of Jesus Christ. All of life needs to be committed unto him. We cannot hold part of our lives for ourselves, but we must be willing as God's children to do everything that the Lord wants us to do. The Bishop of our souls gives us victory in enduring injustice, but the victory will not be realized if we do not let him reign in our lives.

7
Happy Homes

1 Peter 3:1-7

The divorce rate among Americans has increased alarmingly for the last three decades. Divorce has become one of the moral blights of American society. Recently, in one year, there were twice as many homes in the United States destroyed by separation and divorce as were broken by death. This is a tragic fact and reveals that the problem is enormous in its scope, and that there is no easy solution. A well-known physician has said:

Since marriage is common for most people, they should try to make it as congenial and meaningful as possible. Few of those who enter it think of their part in making it a positive relationship. They usually think of what they can obtain from it rather than what they can put into it. Consequently, with so much ignorance on the part of both sexes of what their partner wants and needs, it is small wonder they fail each other and fight more than they enjoy each other.[1]

Hundreds of books have been written by marriage counselors on the problems of marriage relationships and their solutions. Every conceivable problem and every conceivable answer has been suggested and exhaustively discussed. But the never-ending parade to the divorce court goes on. Even worse than this, the majority of married couples today are having difficulties. Though not all of those marriages will end in divorce court, many homes are unhappy because husbands and wives are not getting along with each other.

Consequently the personalities of the children of those homes are being woefully affected.

I once met a man who was the most socially maladjusted person I had every known. He was almost completely hostile. His parents were divorced when he was five years old, but their marriage had been unstable from his birth. He remembered violent arguments in which his mother pleaded with his father to spend more time at home. The father refused, and one day he left for good, without explanation. This twenty-seven-year-old man felt he was to blame for his father's actions, for his mother's miseries, and his grandmother's hatred. Although this experience had taken place in his first five years, this young man was psychologically scarred for life.

The problems in marriage are so numerous that it would be impossible for us to even consider them. Couples are arguing over money, houses, children, jobs, time, authority, sex, social standing, friends, and hundreds of other things.

Most marriage counselors try to solve the problems of unhappy homes by attacking each problem that can be brought out into the open. I believe, however, that all of the problems of marriage can be traced to their source in the souls of the individuals. Recently a psychiatrist wrote about an interview with one of his patients who was having serious mental problems. This patient was divorced but refused to discuss it with the psychiatrist. The reason for the woman's refusal was finally traced to her feeling of failure. She said that she could find hundreds of reasons to give her friends for her divorce, but the real truth of the matter was that both she and her husband were failures in marriage. Many who are married may feel successful. Most couples do not plan a divorce, will make the most of it, but isn't there more that could be found to make marriages better?

There is an answer. God does not give a list of do's and don'ts for the married couple, but he does suggest the secrets to a happy home. These suggestions are made to us in the passage of Scripture under consideration. We cannot separate our thinking from the historical context of the passage. Women had a place of vague inferiority in the social composition of both Jewish and Greek society. The women were to remain silent and at home. Peter realized that some women who had come to Jesus had husbands who remained in paganism. Since the husband was the complete ruler of the house, this could bring about some very serious home problems. Peter told the women that they had to become all they could be spiritually in order to cope with this problem.

Here are the three principles Peter stressed: The lovely life is a witness to all; proper inward adornment is always winning; and there is true togetherness in the loving grace of God. These three principles worked in the age of the New Testament, and they will still serve to create happy homes. In the passage which we consider, the first two of these ideas were applied to a woman who was married to an unbelieving husband. The third idea was applied to the husband. There is a basic underlying principle in all three of these ideas. The ability to attain true happiness at home is within both the husband and the wife of any marriage. Today every husband and wife needs to examine his or her life in light of these three principles. No marriage manual that has been written will give any instruction that is more primary than the three ideas expressed in 1 Peter 3:1-7.

The Silent Witness of a Lovely Life

The silent witness of a lovely life is the theme of verses 1 and 2. In these two verses, Peter was saying to Christian women who have unbelieving husbands that if they would be submissive to their own husbands and exemplify purity and reverence, the silent witness of such a lovely life would ultimately win the husband to a knowledge of Jesus. Not only would such a life win a husband to the knowledge of Jesus Christ but also such a life would command respect from any husband.

Submissiveness is the first mark of a lovely life that will bear its silent witness. Peter simply said, "In like manner, wives, be in subjection to your own husbands; that, even if they obey not the word, they may without the word be gained by the behavior of their wives" (v. 1). The expression "in like manner" refers to 2:18. In the same way that Peter instructed slaves to be in subjection to their masters, he instructs wives to be submissive to their husbands. Paul gave similar instruction to wives. Neither Paul nor Peter were asking wives to do something that is impossible to do. Both were saying that wives are to submit themselves to their own husbands as an expression of love. Paul said, "Wives obey your husbands" (5:22); he also said, "Husbands, love your wives" (5:25). It is not difficult for a woman to submit herself in total love to a husband who respects her with his own total love.

There is objectiveness and subjectiveness on the parts of both husband and wife in the matter of submissiveness. Any husband who would take advantage of the submissiveness of his wife is demonstrating that he does not love her with the respect that godly love demands. A godly wife, who loves her husband with all of her heart and submits herself to him as a wife should, can win the total respect of her husband in physical, intellectual, emotional, and spiritual matters. A godly man, who loves his wife to the degree that he receives such submissiveness from her, will also be able to win his wife physically, intellectually, emotionally, and spiritually.

Purity is the second jewel of loveliness that witnesses to an unbelieving partner. Peter said that the Christian wife will be able to witness to her unbelieving husband when he beholds her chaste or pure manner of life. The purity of which the Lord is speaking may be applied just as well to a husband of an unbelieving wife. The Lord is saying that if any Christian is married to an unbeliever, he or she will be able to win that unbeliever to a knowledge of Jesus by showing the purity of the Christian spirit in the total way of his or her life.

Many people think that they can win their unbelieving partners by compromising with them. Often a Christian woman who is married to an unbeliever will participate in his unchristian conduct, thinking that this will ultimately win his respect. No Christian ever wins the respect of an unbeliever by compromise. When one knows the life of another, as husbands and wives do, any impurities of faith can be recognized. The Lord, therefore, expects the Christian to do what is right in every respect before his or her unbelieving wife or husband. The lovely life that is totally committed to the Lord and directed by him in its conduct will be a winning life.

Though we are going beyond the teaching of 1 Peter, it seems fair to say that the same purity of life would be expected of any husband or wife married to a believer. Full respect for each other will not be realized until they observe purity in the other's faith. This same purity is the only hope that the world will ultimately respect that life. A Christian home ought to be a witnessing home, and it will be a witnessing home if all the members of the household show the pure lives that God expects.

Peter said that the lovely life that truly witnesses is one that reverences God. This reverence for God is more than an occasional glance toward heaven or a tip of the hat to the Scriptures. It is a fear which respects God as he reveals himself. Such reverence does not seek to recreate God as one wants him to be, but it is a reverence which submits the entire life unto the Lord. With this kind of reverence, one's religion becomes a total way of life. Men and women give themselves entirely unto the Lord. This means that their conduct and problems are committed to the Lord. Christians will be obedient to the commands of the Lord in their home relationships. Any wife or husband who has this respect for God will likely have an influence over every member of the household. This kind of reverent life will be a witness for Jesus Christ.

The Salient Wooing of a Lovely Spirit

The salient wooing of a lovely spirit is expressed in Peter's description of the inward adornment of the Christian woman (vv. 3-6). Few passages in all of the Bible so vividly describe and stress the true value of the beauty of the inward Christian life.

Verse 3 reminds one of Isaiah 3:16-24. In this passage Isaiah said that the women of Israel would be a part of the judgment of God because they had improperly valued the outward expressions of human beauty. Peter seemed to be emphasizing the same thing. He said that the adorning of a witnessing Christian woman was not to be judged by outward appearance. Peter was not putting value on unattractiveness, but he was saying that if the outward appearance is all that is stressed one misses the mark. He said that the hairstyle, jewelry, and clothing are not the important things. He was not saying that a woman should let her hair look like semi-wet spaghetti, nor is she to wear shabby clothing. The coiffure and the clothing, however, are not to be the important things. There is a higher function in life than outward appearance. The inner life is much more important. The adornment of the inner person ought to receive the primary attention of every Christian.

Peter said that the attitude of the heart is important (v. 4). One should dress in a meek and quiet spirit. Every deed performed proceeds from the spirit or inward self. Many people try to be one thing on the outside but are something else on the inside. We do not really fool ourselves when we live with such hypocrisy. A few people who do not know us very well may be fooled for awhile, but we do not fool the people who are with us day-by-day. Ultimately what is on the inside will come out.

If we want our lives to be right with one another at home, then we must put on the meekness and quietness of the spirit of Jesus Christ himself. No husband or wife can be happy at home if their love and conduct of love is only an outward expression. For real lasting happiness the expressions of love must be born out of the inward spirit. In the last phrase of verse 4, Peter said that such an inward spirit, which is meek and quiet because of its relationship to God, is a thing of great value in the sight of God.

Verses 5-6 illustrate this point. Peter said that Sarah was a woman who had a pure heart. She did not have to fight with herself to respect her husband and call him lord. She did this because she wanted to, and she wanted to because she had God in her heart.

Many husbands and wives today seek to find little ways to be nice to each other on the outside in order to get along, but inwardly there is constant conflict. This conflict could be solved and real happiness of life could be found if husbands and wives would put on the inward apparel of meek and quiet spirits.

The Sharing Ways of Loving Grace

The sharing ways of loving grace are the emphases of verse 7. Peter instructed husbands to "dwell with your wives according to knowledge, giving honor unto the woman, as unto the weaker vessel, as being also joint-heirs of the grace of life; to the end that your prayers be not hindered." There are two very important points for husbands to remember in their relationship to their wives.

The first of these is that women are the weaker vessels, according to Peter. There is a disagreement today concerning the meaning of "weaker vessel." In terms of physical strength, women are usually seen as weaker than men. However, in terms of survival, male babies have a higher mortality rate. Some also understand "weaker vessel" to indicate the lack of social standing of women in Peter's day. However, there are physical reasons for women to be dependent upon men. This dependence, however, does not give men any spiritual superiority.

The second fact that is stated in this passage is that women are equal with men spiritually. They are "joint heirs of the grace of life." This fact, which was first taught by Jesus, has changed the whole course of the world. This truth has also made it possible for men and women to live together in this world in true happiness. Though women are dependent upon men for many things, they are spiritual equals. This demands that husband and wife will respect each other.

Many people have not learned these two points, and consequently they have not been able to find spiritual happiness at home. There are women who absolutely refuse to admit that they are the weaker sex in any sense. They do not wish to have any dependence upon their husbands. The result is the relationship is less than God desires.

There are also men who refuse to look upon women as their spiritual equals. Because a man is stronger physically, and often the family depends upon him for means of support, he does not see that his wife shares equally in the grace of life that God has given. Consequently he does not have for her the fullest mental and spiritual respect that he ought to have.

Peter said that the result of such disrespect on the part of a husband and wife will bring about a hindrance to their prayers. The spiritual life of the home is endangered by improper respect for each other. Husbands and wives need to respect each other for what they are physically and for what God has made them spiritually.

In the grace of God, there is a sharing of responsibility. The wife who knows the grace of God respects the place of leadership which belongs to her husband. She is willing to depend upon him in physical matters and to follow his leadership in spiritual matters, when he is a Christian. The husband who knows God also respects his wife as a gift from God. He respects her as God has made her. To respect her as the weaker sex means that he will respect her feelings. He will not seek to use her simply for his own gratification. But out of love, he will respect every attitude and emotion which she possesses. It means that he will expect her to share with him the great things that God gives in grace. The faith of the husband and the wife ought to be a united faith which stands before God as one. When this is the case, there is no insurmountable problem ever to be faced. The home that is built upon the loving grace of God is a home that has sharing ways.

It is certainly true that there are many home problems today, just as there were home problems in the first century. Our problems today may be different than were the problems spoken of by Simon Peter, but the principles which he teaches are still the answers to many of our needs. The lovely life will always be a silent witness through the power of the Holy Spirit in any home. The inward adornment of a lovely spirit will silently woo the heart of any person who lives in the home. When two Christians share their lives with each other in a husband and wife relationship, there will be sharing ways born out of the possession of the loving grace of God which they have through Jesus.

If you have not been happy in the past in your home relationships, will you let these principles be applied to you? In total submission to the Lord, you will find victory at home and you will have a happy home.

Note

1. O. S. English and G. J. Pearson, *Emotional Problems of Living* (New York: W.W. Horton & Co., 1963), pp. 455-456.

8
For the Love of Life

1 Peter 3:8-12

Have you ever noticed that it is very difficult to tell your troubles to another? When I start complaining, I get the impression that my friends are not listening because they cannot wait to tell me their troubles. If I am sick, they are sicker. If I am worried, they have more to worry them.

It is very easy to become negative about life. The theme of the day could be "all is wrong!" Many people are unhappy. They are unhappy about nearly everything. Neighbors are unhappy with one another. Husbands and wives are sad with each other. Children and parents do not understand each other. Communities despair. Churches are shaken by discord. States are jealous of one another. Nations are at war. "Friends" smile at one another face-to-face, then criticize behind backs.

Recently a government official said that most people take vacations, "just to get away from it all." Most people are tired of what they are doing and dislike their way of life, but they proceed with it and continually complain about it.

A young mother went to a counselor to relate to him a very hideous sin she had committed. Her only explanation for playing the complete fool was that she was tired of her ordinary life. It bored her, and she was very unhappy.

A young army man, who had become an alcoholic, was heard to say of his problem, "About the only explanation I have is, I am just tired of living and scared to die." Perhaps he expressed the theme of many people. Because so many people are tired of living, they are taking daring excursions into the unacceptable to try to find happiness. This is the story of the prodigal son in Luke's Gospel. While this boy was at home, happiness was all around him, but all he could think about was something that he wanted. He cried, "Father, give me the goods!" He wanted to move out into the unacceptable to find happiness. Instead of happiness, he found himself in a pigpen.

While visiting Chicago a few years ago, I visited "Skid Row." I waited until after midnight and had a taxi take me from one end to the other. I saw on the street nearly every kind of sin one could imagine. Do you know why? One of the drunken derelicts told me that he was just trying to be happy. Drunkenness, addiction to dope, adultery, robbery, fighting, cursing, hatred, and other sins were all being committed because people were trying to be happy.

Is this the way to be happy? All people want to be happy. People try many things in their quest for happiness: built homes, bought cars and boats, taken trips, and acquired possessions. Instead of happiness, they have found more unhappiness.

Is there not an answer? Of course there is. In 1 Peter 3:8-12, we find an answer. Let us remember that Peter was giving instructions on domestic happiness to a group of persecuted Christians. In 2:18-25, he told slaves how they were to be obedient to their masters and serve God even in oppression. In 3:1-7, he instructed husbands and wives on loving each other and serving God in harmony. In 3:8-12, he concluded this great passage on social ethics by showing how to be happy while living in this world.

Peter was saying that there is a way to "love life, and see good days" (v. 10). It is not necessary to be unhappy and dissatisfied all of the time. In verses 10-12 Peter quoted from Psalm 34. The psalmist said that people can have happy lives if their lives are centered in the Lord. This was a typical idea in Jewish thought. In the apocryphal book of Tobit, Tobit called his son, Tobias, to him and instructed him in some family matters, then he said to him,

"My son, be mindful of the Lord our God all thy days, and let not thy will be set to sin, or to transgress his commandments: do uprightly all thy life long, and follow not the ways of unrighteousness. For if thou deal truly, thy doings shall prosperously succeed to thee and to all them that live justly" (Tobit 4:5-6).

Anyone can have happiness in the Lord. Outside the Lord no person can have happiness. Even in a world of persecution, people of the first century could "love life, and see good days" (v. 10).

Today, in a generation of sin and ungodliness, where all people have so much sorrow, we can "love life, and see good days." To do this, however, we must base our hopes upon the right things. If we are going to seek happiness in the "things of the world," then, like the prodigal, we will come to the pigpen. If we will place our lives with all social obligations in the hands of Jesus Christ, then we can have very happy lives. The verses for our study in this lesson show us how to place our lives ethically with Jesus.

Ethical Obligations

Let us first observe our ethical obligations. Verses 8-9 say that we need to have the right outlook in this matter. This outlook is to be followed by the proper feeling, or attitude, and in turn the proper action toward our fellow human beings will result.

Peter said, "Finally, be ye all like minded" (v. 8). He meant that we are to share a common heritage of faith. The word translated "like minded" appears only this one time in the New Testament, and it means concordant. This is the right attitude in our ethical obligations. Many people are unhappy simply because they are always fractious. Agreement or disagreement is often simply an attitude.

Peter was teaching fellow Christians the attitude they were to possess toward each other. We have a common heritage of faith. We have fellowhip because we have "one faith" in "one Lord." If we love life, we must cease to find reasons to disagree with our fellow Christians. Our despiteful attitudes must be conquered. No matter how many things we may possess in life, if we have contempt toward our fellow human beings, we will be miserable. This is what Paul meant when he said, "Though I speak with the tongues of men and of angels, and have not love, I am become as sounding brass, or a tinkling cymbal" (1 Cor. 13:1).

The desire for unity will bring compassion toward others. This is the second of our ethical obligations. So long as prime importance is placed on self, sympathy cannot exist. In Romans 12:15, Paul exhorted Christians to "rejoice with them that do rejoice, and weep with them that weep." This is true sympathy. When such rapport is established with other Christians, then we have real sympathy. If we tune our lives to the feelings of others, we will be useful in God's service. If we would love life, our lives must be useful.

The Bible teaches that the church is the body of Christ. As such, it is like a human body with many members. Every member of the human body is related. When one part suffers, all suffer. "And whether one member suffer, all the members suffer with it; or one member be honoured, all the members rejoice with it" (1 Cor. 12:26, KJV). Real sympathy does mean that we feel the pains of others. It also means that we rejoice in another's victories.

Perhaps it is easier to sympathize in agony than it is to empathize in happiness. To have real rejoicing over the good fortune of another means that all covetousness and jealousy must be conquered. No matter how successful we are, if we do not overcome feelings which degrade us, we cannot be happy. On the other hand, no matter how little we have, if we can truly rejoice in the good things that comes to another, then we can be happy. If we would enjoy life, we should try sympathy. It may be that we will feel wanted and needed for the first time in life as the result of this new attitude.

As a result of our acceptance of an outlook of like-mindedness and a feeling of sympathy, there will come new action in our lives. The first noticeable action that will be seen is kindness. Kindness grows out of real love. One who is sympathetic out of love will be kind. Peter simply stated that we are to be "loving as brethren" (v. 8). If we applied real family love to every decision and deed of life, the result would be kindness in all of our dealings.

When are we the most unhappy? Usually it is when we are in conflict with our fellowman. When a neighbor, business associate, friend, or family member is unhappy with us; then we are sad and depressed. Jesus taught that if we would return kindness ultimately happiness would come to us. Kindness will always overcome. Many people do not believe this. They put on a big show, trying to prove that they are unkind and that they are successful because of it. Inwardly they are depressed, sad, and miserable. Nothing will substitute for the kindness of family love to cause us to love life.

Humility is the next act of life that will show itself in one's ethical obligations. Many people have forgotton that humility is a virtue. Some people in religious work have forgotten the virtue of humility. Many have adopted certain promotional schemes, thinking that if they promote themselves they will succeed in doing things for God. They may do bigger things, but there is a question concerning for whom these things are done. If service is without humility, it is obviously being done for one's own benefit.

The humility that is mentioned here is "humbleminded-ness." This means that one will see himself as God created him, as a *part* of a world with other people. If one is really humbleminded, then she will not be "rendering evil for evil, or reviling for reviling; but contrariwise bless;.ıg" (v. 9). The act of humility is more than thinking that we are lowly people. It is properly evaluating ourselves in relation to those with whom we have dealings. It is going beyond the ordinary response that is expected by the world in human relations.

Again we are reminded of the teaching of Jesus in the Sermon on the Mount. When one mistreats us, we are to overcome evil with good. This is what Jesus meant when he said to turn the other cheek and go the second mile. It is easy to return evil for evil, but the only way to render good for evil is to commit ourselves entirely to the Lord. In this humble submission, God will win these victories for us. In humble submission is real happiness because this is the way that God intended life to be.

God's children are called to this kind of humility. A call to everlasting life is a call to God's way of life. When we answer this call, we "inherit a blessing," blessings of his presence and fellowship. We do not have to defend and vindicate ourselves when the Lord is with us.

It is fitting to obey these ethical obligations in outlook, feeling, and action for the love of life. People cannot realize even a small portion of their potential in satisfaction until they accept their ethical obligations.

Ego Abdication

In verses 10-11 we observe that there must be ego abdication for the love of life. No one can really measure up to his potential until he abdicates himself to God. Jesus said, "If any man will come after me, let him deny himself, and take up his cross, and follow me" (Matt. 16:24). Peter was saying that to live with other people and enjoy life as God intended, Christians must deny themselves. Peter expressed this self-denial in very practical terms.

The first step of ego abdication is to control the tongue. Immediately we remember the words of James. He said,

The tongue is a fire, a world of iniquity; so is the tongue among our members, that it defileth the whole body, and setteth on fire the course of nature; and it is set on fire of hell. For every kind of beasts, and of birds, and of serpents, and of things in the sea, is tamed, and hath been tamed of mankind: But the tongue can no man tame, it is an unruly evil, full of deadly poison (Jas. 3:6-8, KJV).

But to have life, which means enjoy life, we must learn to refrain our tongues from evil. To refrain the tongue from evil means to avoid profanity, slander, and lying; but it certainly means more than this.

It is always an act of courtesy to avoid profanity and excess in expression. Courtesy also demands that unkind expressions be put aside.

Christians, however, are admonished to go beyond the demands of simple courtesy. We are to get control of our hearts which control our tongues. James indicated that the heart is important in the control of the tongue. He said, "If any man among you seem to be religious, and bridleth not his tongue, but deceiveth his own heart; this man's religion is vain" (1:26). If people have real religion, they have Christ in their hearts. Inability to control one's tongue indicates that Christ is not in a person's heart. Commitment to Christ is something that needs to be done every day. While it is true that the commitment of faith for salvation is a once-for-all act, it is also true that the faith that overcomes in the daily problems of life is a day-by-day commitment to the Lord.

To find the happy life, we must not only learn to control our tongues but we must also turn away from evil deeds. Peter simply said, "Let him turn away from evil, and do good" (v. 11). There is progression in the idea. One does not use pious words and then do evil things, but one avoids evil deeds as well as evil talk. The tenses of the verbs indicate that the action of turning away from evil and doing good is to be a very decisive act.

Peter made the important suggestion that good is to fill the vacuum which is created when one turns away from evil. Many people have grave problems with this. They want to have good lives, knowing that requires turning away from evil. When they have turned from evil, they become critical and self-righteous. The problem is that they have not filled their lives with good. We must be positive. The way to be positive is to turn the deeds of life over to Jesus Christ. He will not only show what good needs to be done but also he gives the strength to do the good deeds. We must make ourselves available to him. Paul, in agreement with this idea, said, "I beseech you therefore, brethren, by the mercies of God, that you present your bodies a living sacrifice, holy, acceptable unto God, which is your reasonable service" (Rom. 12:1, KJV).

The third aspect of ego abdication is the pursuit of peace. Before peace can be pursued, it must be sought. Peter said, "Let him seek peace and pursue it" (v. 11, RSV). In the midst of their suffering, these Christians were to flee to the Giver of peace as their refuge. These "strangers" were not to forget that they were the "elect" of God. In this there was peace. If we seek to make peace ourselves, it will not be peace. Today we need to seek peace in Jesus. Real peace can only be found in him. We must "deny ourselves" and claim only Jesus in our hearts, as the means of spiritual satisfaction and peace. Having sought out this peace, we must then pursue it every day at all cost. If the believers will stay with the Prince of Peace, no matter how much suffering comes, their soul will be at peace. Christians will also spread peace to others because they know and associate with the Giver of real spiritual peace.

If you would love life, then rest your heart in the sweet peace of Jesus and follow every moment of every day in the path of the Master of peace.

Eternal Observation

If we would love life, we must remember that we are under eternal observation. Peter said, "For the eyes of the Lord are upon the righteous, and his ears unto their supplication: but the face of the Lord is upon them that do evil" (v. 12). Two very precious promises and a grave and challenging warning are in this verse.

First Peter was saying that no deed of righteousness ever done by the children of God goes without the notice of God. The Christians of the first century were gravely persecuted, but God told them to give back good for the evil they had received. This was the pursuit of peace. The world could scorn them for this, but God would see and bless. What greater reward could anyone have than to know that the approving eye of God is upon him or her? No matter how bad secular life may seem, this look of divine approval makes life worth living. Certainly, no matter how good physical life might be, it would be very empty and futile apart from God's approval. In this strange pilgrimage upon which God sets his family of children, he does not forsake us; but he says, "Lo, I am with you alway" (Matt. 28:20, KJV).

Besides looking upon us with his wonderful grace, God listens to us when we talk to him. The most wonderful experiences possible have been mine as a Christian because God has listened when I prayed. We know that we are not forsaken in this journey of faith because our Father listens and answers when we leave our burdens with him. At every moment of discouragement, we can talk to God; he will listen and answer. Jesus said, "Ask, and it shall be given you; seek, and ye shall find; knock, and it shall be opened unto you" (Matt. 7:7, KJV). Life is worth living in fellowship with a loving Heavenly Father who watches over us, listens to our needs, and answers when we talk to him.

God also vindicates his people against those who stand against them. This is what Peter meant when he said, "The face of the Lord is against them that do evil" (v. 12, KJV). There is a certain unique persistence about the children of God. As they walk in fellowship with him they understand what he means when he says of the church, "The gates of hell shall not prevail against it" (Matt. 16:18, KJV). God keeps his people in his hand. They may suffer physically, but God will not let spiritual violence overtake them. To live with God is really living.

If you would love life and see good days, you will have to do it God's way. Suffering is real and cannot be denied. God does not say to deny it. Instead he shows us how to live with it. Accept your ethical obligations. Be willing to abdicate self. Live under the eternal observation of God. This is life at its best.

9
Songs for the Journey

1 Peter 3:13-17

What a friend we have in Jesus,
All our sins and griefs to bear
· ·
Precious Savior, still our refuge;
Take it to the Lord in prayer.

In these times when sin is so evident, people need a Savior to forgive them. In these impersonal days, they need a friend who is true. We have many needs our Friend and Savior can supply.

We need comfort for our troubled hearts. Some have experienced tragic trials. Some have lost loved ones to death. Others have loved ones suffering, and death is coming.

We need rest for weary bodies. Some have labored long and hard in their pilgrimages of life, working from morning till night, and the rewards have been hard to find.

We sometimes feel unwanted and useless. Some have decided that their time of usefulness is past. Some need a purpose to give a new guideline to life.

We need care in physical agony. There are backaches, arthritis, sore feet, weak eyes, wounded hearts, and disabled bodies.

We sometimes feel the pressures of financial burdens. There is not enough money to pay all of the bills—to clothe, feed, house, and educate the family. These days of inflation impose great needs.

We need to feel loved. Some are lonely. Loved ones are gone and, after years of sacrifice, the joy of companionship that you expected has fled.

In these times there are great needs. Trouble is everywhere. Most headlines in every newspaper are startling. War, crime, greed, hate are running wild.

Perhaps we could ask, "Is there no song for the journey?" The tempo of our age seems to be set by the twitching of nerves under stress. A song with that tempo makes the journey more burdensome. Is there no song for us that exclaims an answer to our needs?

A great poet of Israel said, "Thy statutes have been my songs in the house of my pilgrimage" (Ps. 119:54, KJV). This poet lived in a time when God's people had to suffer. The proud ways of the world had sorely tempted the writer of this psalm; but through "the night," he remembered the name of the Lord (Ps. 119:55). The psalmist had troubles, needs, but he had an answer to his needs in the Lord.

Christ is the answer to every need that we have. Dr. Edwin McNeely said that Christ was a song for this age:

Christ's life on earth was a symphony of harmonic beauty. The *tempo* of his birth changed the patter of peace; the *doloroso* of His humiliation shows the way of meekness; the *sfrozondo* of His death on the cross made eternal salvation come nigh; the *fortissimo* of His resurrection is heard in glad hallelujahs around the earth; the *crescendo* of the Gospel story is heard every hour; the *finale* in the *dal segno. Atonality* is known in the life of Christ. No *discordant triad* ever sounded in his teachings.[1]

Christ in us is a triumphant hallelujah chorus. He is the song for our pilgrimage here.

Peter knew that there would be occasion for suffering and trial for every Christian. In 1 Peter 3:13 to 5:11, Peter talked about the trials of the Christian life. He encouraged his readers to endure their trials with courage. He told them that Christ endured the suffering of the cross. As the suffering Savior, he is the victory for all Christians in the times of need. Peter was saying that the dirge of our times can be turned to a song for our pilgrimage if we will let Christ reign in our lives.

Christ Is a Protective Song

As a boy, I whistled while walking down a lonely path at night. I was not whistling my song to frighten away any unseen enemy, but to comfort my frightened emotions. Jesus can calm our frightened hearts today. Certainly there are many reasons for being afraid in today's world. Foreign affairs are explosive. Domestic problems are disturbing. Morals are at a low ebb. Religion is often held in lowest esteem. Some people of God are imprisoned. Others have been put to death. The political elements of our world are frightening.

The lethargy of our own people, which has lulled us into the greatest era of decline in religious activities that we have ever known, is frightening. Ministers are preaching against the menace of mediocrity. Church leaders throughout the world are begging for people to have a compassionate concern, but no change is evident. This lethargy is frightening.

We are frightened by our own personal problems. Many of our problems have no easy or apparent answers. We cannot see how to overcome them. What will we do?

Verse 13 says, "Who is he that will harm you, if ye be zealous of that which is good?" Peter was saying that if Christians become zealous for goodness, the protective hand of the Lord will be upon them. Peter was not saying that there is no one who would harm people in well doing, but those who would are the enemies of God. Since they are not on the Lord's side, the enemies of God may try to harm God's people; but ultimately the enemies will fail. Apparently there were people who were doing great physical harm to the Christians who first received Peter's message. Peter was not very concerned about physical harm because he felt that there was something more important.

Paul said, "If God be for us, who can be against us? He that spared not his own Son, but delivered him up for us all, how shall he not with him also freely give us all things?" (Rom. 8:31-32, KJV). Like Peter, Paul was not saying that bad things cannot happen to saved people. He was saying that God can even bless his people in bad things.

Perhaps there is a subjective thought here which is very important. In zeal for goodness, there is protection from harm. While assaults may come to the Christian in one's zeal for goodness, one will see the victory that goodness brings. I once asked a well-known evangelist if he were ever abused in his efforts in soul winning. He smilingly told me of threatenings, cursings, dismissals, and other abuses. I asked him why he was smiling. He said that he was happy that he had been given the privilege of trying to witness to these people. Their rejection of him made him unhappy, but the fact that the Lord had led him to go to them made him happy.

This is the kind of protective song that the Lord will put in his people's hearts. He will not keep them from physical harm, but he will find a way to bless them even while they are being harmed. No abuse is really important while the Lord is present with his children to heal their wounds.

Christ Is a Happy Song

The songs that God's children sing are happy songs. In verse 14 Peter said, "But if you should suffer because of righteousness, be happy, and fear not their fear, neither be afraid." Of course, the previous verse is better understood in light of this verse. The harm that people inflict is not very hurtful when one is "happy" in the Lord.

This is reminiscent of one of the Beatitudes of Jesus. He said, "Blessed are they which are persecuted for righteousness' sake: for their's is the kingdom of heaven" (Matt. 5:10, KJV). The suffering that people would inflict upon the Christian who is serving the Lord would be "because of righteousness." The Lord commands his people to be happy if they are suffering for doing what is right. Rather than adding to your woes the agony of self-inflicted punishment, be happy while people speak out against you for your Christian stand.

There are many reasons to be happy for the Christian who suffers for the Lord's sake. Acts tells of the abuses that the apostles suffered for their preaching. They were beaten and commanded not to speak in the name of Jesus. "They departed from the presence of the council, rejoicing that they were counted worthy to suffer shame for his name" (Acts 5:41). The Lord had been with these faithful men even as they suffered for him. They loved Jesus so much that they rejoiced that they had the privilege of sharing in his suffering. We can rejoice in suffering for his sake, if we love him. There is happiness rather than sorrow in sharing the afflictions of Jesus.

The Christian can rejoice in suffering because he is having fellowship with Jesus as he suffers. The Lord completed our salvation through suffering. The nature of Christ made him a contradiction to the world. It was absolutely essential for him to suffer. This has already been discussed in an earlier chapter. It is sufficient to say that the Christian can have happiness even in suffering, when he knows that he is sharing the cross of Jesus.

The third reason to be happy is expressed in the last part of the verse. "Fear not their fear, neither be afraid." This is a part of a quotation from Isaiah 8:12-13. In that passage, Isaiah was probably exhorting his people to have no fear of the king of Assyria. They were not to be afraid of the disaster which seemed to be impending, but they were to trust the Lord to take care of them. Therefore, Peter was saying that Christians who are persecuted for righteousness sake should not be afraid of their persecutors, but they should trust the Lord. With trust in the Lord, one can be happy while one suffers. The happy song of faith comforts the suffering child of God.

Whatever our problems, if we trust the Lord while we suffer, he will put a happy song in our lives.

Christ Is a Hopeful Song

Hopeful songs will be ours while we suffer if we make Christ the Lord in our lives. The key to overcoming the heavy burdens of life is to let Christ reign as the Lord of life. Peter said, "But sanctify in your hearts Christ as Lord, ready always to give an answer to all who seek from you word concerning the hope in you; but with meekness and fear, having a good conscience, that in whatever things you are abused, they may be put to shame, who revile the good manner of your life in Christ" (vv. 15-16).

It is important for a person to say that Christ is the Savior, but it is equally important to sanctify him as the Lord of her heart. Actually, it is not possible to claim Jesus as Savior without claiming him as Lord. The key to victory in suffering is to let him be Lord. The hope of victory in the time of suffering cannot be realized until the entire life is given to him as Lord.

The hope that is born in the heart of the Christian, who has sanctified Christ as Lord, will do three things. It will give an answer concerning the reason of hope, it will give a good conscience, and it will put opponents to shame.

If Christ reigns as Lord in our lives, we have an answer to all who seek from us words concerning our hope. The world cannot understand how one can suffer and be happy in that suffering. A young mother of our church who was about to die, and suffering greatly in her sickness, wrote the following words:

> As I traveled down the long long road,
> My burdens became a heavy load.
> I thought my faith beyond compare,
> But the blessed Lord put a burden there.
> Amidst my pain and agony,

I cried, Oh Lord, why me?
Have I not proved my faith to thee?
Then the Savior answered me:
Did I not bear my cross in shame?
Don't, dear child, question my name.
Lifting my face up to the sky
I cried, Oh Lord, here am I.
My faith had vanished like winter snow,
Melting as the burdens did grow.
Now, I know what a blessing I hold,
As he to his bosom my soul does fold.

Ann Harrelson wrote these words a few days before she died. None of the family and the hospital staff could understand how this young woman could happily suffer so much. The poem tells how. She had sanctified Christ as the Lord. He had become the reason for hope. She was ready to sing in the choirs of heaven, and she knew it. While she suffered, she was singing the song of hope.

Christ the Lord is the answer to all questions concerning the hope that is in every Christian. The Lord will strengthen us for the hardships of the present life, and then, when it is all finished here, he will take us to heaven. He is our hope.

The second stanza of the song of hope in the Lord is a good conscience. The Christian may suffer for doing what is right and good, but he suffers in meekness and fear. This simply means that he is humble and respects God as the Lord of life. It is not necessary for the Christian to understand suffering. Volume upon volume has been written to try to explain suffering, but it all fails. One who meekly trusts the Lord does not find it necessary to have an explanation. His hope is in the Lord. If suffering is his lot, then God will take care of him. This is the good conscience.

This kind of hope in the Lord will actually put to shame all who revile the good manner of life that God's child has. The

Christian does not have to fight against those who cause her to suffer. Her trust in the Lord is sufficient.

The theme of our song of hope is the lordship of Christ. With meekness and respect, we trust him to reign over us. Christ the Lord is our hope.

What is your trouble? What burden do you carry? As you journey through this life as a stranger and a pilgrim, if you will let Christ rule every thought, deed, and attitude, he will carry your burden and lift your troubles. There is a song for the journey.

Note

1. Edwin McNeely, *Evangelistic Music* (Fort Worth: Seminary Hill Press, 1959), p. 78.

10
Victorious Salvation

1 Peter 3:18-22

Recently a young man who had belonged to the church for many years came to me to ask how to be saved. He revealed that he had no spiritual joy in his life and was not persuaded that Jesus was the Savior. Since he was not trusting Christ, he felt only misery when he thought about religion. He revealed that he was miserable when attending church or even when talking about religion. He knew a radiant member of our church who seemed to be very happy and confident in the Lord. He said that he would like to trade the kind of experience he had for the kind that brought this radiant victory.

Apparently there are many people who have had the same kind of experience that this young man had—they joined the church but did not join Jesus. I cannot think of anything that would be more demanding on one's conscience than affiliation with a church without having the Savior in one's heart.

As we have seen throughout this study, life has many trials for the real Christian. For one who only claims to be a Christian, it must be unbearable. Peter wanted us to know, however, that there is real victorious salvation even for sufferers in Christ. When we suffer for our faith, we are doing exactly what Christ did in our behalf. "It is better to suffer for well doing" (v. 17). Both the saved and the unsaved suffer; but for the saved, the victory has been won by the Lord which gives them joy in suffering. There is a victorious salvation that makes life worth living, no matter what any or all of the external circumstances might be.

Adoniram Judson deteriorated in prison in Burma, but he rejoiced as he starved because he had a victorious salvation. Bill Wallace died at the hands of the Communists in China, but he died in victory because he was saved. People have endured flames, prisons, lion's dens, jeers, whispers, and every kind of atrocity for serving Jesus; but they have done it victoriously because they were saved.

Has your religion brought real victory to your life? You can have real victory, but you must have it the way God gives it.

The Place of Victory

Victorious salvation will bring us face-to-face with God. Verse 18 says, "For Christ also suffered once concerning sins, the just in behalf of the unjust, in order that he might bring us face-to-face with God, by dying on the one hand in the flesh, but by being made alive on the other hand in the Spirit." The ultimate purpose in the redemptive work of Christ is to bring people face-to-face with God. This means that Christ made it possible for us to be brought into proper relationship with God. Paul called this reconciliation.

People need reconciliation because they are sinners. Many people overlook this very important fact in their religion. Frequently sin is judged by human standards of right and wrong instead of God's standards. Many have tried to take the conscience of sin out of religious experience. However, every sin is against God. Because it is, one cannot have a victorious salvation as long as the blight of sin has not been cured. A person may join the church and act respectably but still be burdened with sin. We cannot come face-to-face with God until something is done about sin.

Only one thing can atone for our sins. "Christ once suffered concerning sins." Until Christ's atonement for sin has been accepted by the individual, that person can have no victory over sin and, consequently, cannot come face-to-face with God.

The suffering that has been done for our sins was done by Christ's death on the cross. Peter said that we are brought face-to-face with God by his dying in the flesh. Although Peter was present at the crucifixion of Christ, he made no attempt to describe its agony, as so many modern preachers do. The suffering Jesus experienced is beyond human comprehension. Peter knew the gory details of the physical suffering of Christ, but he knew that there was something far more important in Christ's death. By dying on the cross in the flesh, Christ won complete victory over sin in the lives of all people who come to God by him.

To mentally minimize sin may placate one's conscience for a short time, but there is no victory in it. The knowledge of guilt returns very soon. There is victory over sin when we accept Christ, who died for our sins in his flesh upon the cross. He did this in perfect justice. "The just for the unjust" is the means of his victory over sin. No martyr could atone for sin because all people are sinful, but Christ knew no sin. He was the one man who died without sin.

Paul belabors this point in Romans 8:1-4.

There is therefore now no condemnation to them which are in Christ Jesus, who walk not after the flesh, but after the Spirit. For the law of the Spirit of life in Christ Jesus hath made me free from the law of sin and death. For what the law could not do, in that it was weak through the flesh, God sending his own Son in the likeness of sinful flesh, and for sin, condemned sin in the flesh: That the righteousness of the law might be fulfilled in us who walked not after the flesh, but after the Spirit (KJV).

Paul said Christ came in the likeness of sinful flesh but

was never a sinner; he was always righteous. Because of this righteousness, Jesus was able to condemn sin in the flesh. He condemned sin by taking it to the cross. It was not his sin that Jesus nailed to the cross, but the sin of the unjust: your sin and mine.

We are unjust, but we are justified through the death of Christ. Paul said, "Therefore being justified by faith, we have peace with God through our Lord Jesus Christ" (Rom. 5:1, KJV). A sinner cannot be brought face-to-face with God until he is justified through the vicarious victory of Jesus by personal faith.

The complete victory of salvation is not fully realized through commitment to the dying Savior. One must add to commitment a complete submission to the living Lord. Peter said, "He died on the one hand in the flesh, but he is made alive on the other hand in the Spirit." A person does not give herself to a dead Christ, but to a living Lord. Many people think of Christ as a nebulous theory, rather than a living Lord. Consequently their religion is a theoretical theology, rather than a way of life in fellowship with God.

Since Christ is made alive, he lives in the hearts of those who really trust him. He is our victory over the principle of sin through his atoning act, and he is our victory over the acts of sin through his living reign as Lord in our hearts. This is the victory that real salvation brings to us. Through fellowship with the living Lord, we are brought to God so that our lives today enjoy the blessings of salvation. Salvation is not just something for the future, but it is living in fellowship with God who is alive in our world today.

Like the Christians of the first century, we are able to endure any hardship with this kind of salvation. We have been brought to God in reconciliation through the suffering of Christ for us on the cross, and we are brought to God in fellowship now through the reign of the resurrected Christ in our hearts.

The Completeness of Victory

The scope of victorious salvation is realized in the unusual revelation in verses 19-20. These verses are highly controversial in their interpretation. The traditional interpretation says that Christ went to hell during the period of time from his death until the resurrection, and preached to the souls of people who were there. He was said to have particularly preached to the antediluvians who were there. John Huxtable expresses the idea very concisely.

St. Peter seeks in the light of this to fill the gap between the death of Christ and Easter Day. He declares that Christ went to preach to the spirits in prison, whom he equates with those who perished in the flood.[1]

Of course, such an interpretation would express a cosmic scope and a persuasive power in the salvation that Christ offers, but it would lead to some very erroneous ideas. Though the English text would readily lead us to this kind of interpretation, the Greek text would not. The word translated "he went" in the English Bible is a participle and should not be given an indicative translation.

Another interpretation that has been frequently set out for this passage is to say that Christ preached to the disobedient people of Noah's day in the spirit through Noah. Those who hold this view say that the spirits were not in prison when Christ preached to them, but that Christ preached to them by his divine nature through Noah. They were detained in prison like fallen angels in the day of Peter. This interpretation would assuredly say that Christ has won a vicarious and victorious salvation for all people of all ages who would believe his preaching.

Another interpretation is set forth by Rendel Harris and has been accepted by others since him.

The difficulty involved in this passage arises from the fact the

subject by the word ἐκήρυξεν has dropped out of the text, and the name that should be put there is Enoch and not Christ. If Enoch were included the text would appear as:
ΕΝΩΚΑΙ (ΕΝΩΚ) ΤΟΙΧΕΝΦΥΛΑΚΗ
It is the simplest kind of error to change repeated letters in this way![2]

This interesting conjecture certainly would solve the problems involved. But in biblical interpretations, we are not seeking to solve problems but to understand the real meaning of the message. I find it necessary to dismiss this interpretation as conjecture.

E. G. Selwyn says that the passage means that Christ preached to certain "archetypal spirits of evil whose rebellion led to the wickedness which brought about the flood."[3] He says that through his suffering and resurrection Christ made proclamation to certain powers of evil. He says, "From the standpoint of the doctrine of the atonement, the doctrine of Christ's Descent into hell is a pictorial representation of the *utterness* of His victory over sin and death."[4]

The victory of Christ over sin is a complete victory. It is a victory for all who will be persuaded by his preaching. It is this kind of victory because it is a victory over the principle of sin. In the crucifixion, Satan did his worst. He persuaded men to kill Jesus. But Jesus, by dying in the flesh and living in the Spirit, brought victory for all who would believe on him by conquering the forces of evil. His victory over sin is a victory for all people of all ages who believe on him.

The persuasion of God is the death and resurrection of Christ. There is no more persuasive power than this. No amount of religious fervor could atone for the sin of humanity. The death of Jesus was the requirement for atonement. He did conquer sin and all of its consequences through his death and subsequent resurrection. This is sufficient for everyone. Christ has won a complete victory. The forces of evil are conquered for all who believe on him.

The Personality of Victory

The complete victory that Christ has won through his suffering is personally felt through the presence of Christ in our lives now. By this personal presence, he clears our consciences of the guilt of sin.

Eight souls were saved in Noah's ark. They were saved from the water because they had believed the preaching of Noah. Peter said that baptism is a *like* symbol of salvation. When we believe the gospel of Christ and commit ourselves through faith to him, he wins the victory for us personally over the guilt of sin. This cleanses our consciences. Baptism symbolizes our commitment to him as the one who died in the flesh but was raised in the Spirit. Our baptism says that we have been raised with him. If we are raised with him, he lives within us. The life that he lives within us is complete victory because he is completely victorious. Verse 22 says, "Who [Christ] is on the right hand of God, having gone into heaven; angels, and authorities, and powers having been put under his command." This verse is not talking about something that Christ will be but what he already is. He is now reigning in heaven.

When Christians are baptized, they confess that Christ is personally present in their lives. It is wonderful that Christ is now on the right hand of the Father making intercession in our behalf. We may suffer in this life, but the interceding Jesus will take care of our needs. While he is present with the Father he is also present in our lives.

Angels, authorities, and powers are now under Christ. This simply means that any authority that exists is under his power. The authorities of heaven and earth must obey his commands. What a victory this is! Christ lives in us and already every angel, every earthly ruler, and every natural force must obey him. Even if physical life collapses around us, we know that all will be well because the victorious Christ lives in our lives. We will fail in the future as we have in the past, but Christ will never fail. The salvation that we have is not the result of our success, but it is his success. He lives in our lives since he has entered our hearts through faith. He is our victory, so the victory is complete. The personal presence of Jesus Christ in the human life in the salvation experience is the most unique and powerful thing that God has done in the world. In Christ, we cannot lose. He is our victory, so salvation is complete in him.

Through his death and resurrection, Christ brings us face-to-face with God. His redemptive act, which is declared in the gospel, is the persuasive power of salvation. No force greater than the message of his death and resurrection brought by the Holy Spirit can be applied. The salvation accomplished by his death and resurrection is an experience of the personal presence of Jesus in the human life. Through this presence he conquers all of the forces of evil for us. Praise, God, what a Savior!

Notes

1. John Huxtable, "I Peter III 13—Iv 19," British Weekly, CXXXII (April 10, 1952), p. 5.

2. J. Rendel Harris, "A Further Note on the Use of Enoch in I Peter," The Expositor, IV (1901), pp. 346-349.

3. E. G. Selwyn, The First Epistle of St. Peter (London: The St. Martin, 1946), p. 126.

4. Ibid., p. 360.

11
A Victorious Attitude

1 Peter 4:1-11

Attitudes are as varying as are the colors of the rainbow. Often when three people respond to the same stimuli, they respond with three different attitudes. Response will always depend on the facts that have created a point of view. I preached a sermon on heaven to a congregation during a revival. I heard one college student say that heaven is not important, the things of life that are going on now are the important things. A woman, whose husband died just a few weeks before, said that it was a great comfort to her to know that her husband had gone to a wonderful place. Another woman, whose daughter had died a few weeks earlier, said that she could hardly stay in the service. She said that it made her recall the death of her child, and she wanted to forget it as soon as possible.

All three people heard the same words, but each had a different attitude about what was said. The student had come to church with his mind set on action. He didn't want to think about anything that did not call for activity. The widow believed that the biblical revelation about heaven spoke to her because she felt that her husband was there. The mother wanted to refuse to face the reality of her child's death.

Nearly every experience of life will invite different attitudes from the people who are involved. Peter knew that the children of God would suffer. First-century Christians suffered persecution. We suffer many anguishes today as the people of Christ. Peter commanded, "Therefore as Christ suffered in the flesh, equip yourselves with the same attitude, because the one suffering in the flesh has ceased from sin" (v. 1). The command is to equip ourselves with the same attitude that Christ had when he suffered. The word which is translated *attitude* is usually translated *mind* or *thought*. It means mental response. The mental response, or attitude, of Christ toward suffering is plainly revealed in the Bible. Jesus in the garden asked that the suffering be removed; but knowing that the cross was the will of God, he committed himself to suffering.

We must face realities of life *now.* We cannot deny that suffering is real. Let us get our attitudes right so that we can be victorious in the difficult times of life.

The Basis of Attitude

There are two wills to be considered in seeking the attitude of victory in suffering. As has already been stated, Christ gave himself to the will of God when he suffered. The writer of Hebrews said of Christ, "Lo, I come to do thy will, O God" (Heb. 10:9). Peter said that we, like Christ, should give ourselves to the will of God, "that you live no longer in the lusts of men, but in the will of God for the rest of your time in the flesh." This passage reveals three things about the will of God: it is a holy way, even in suffering; it is a way to be taken for the rest of time; and it is a strange way to the world.

In taking the attitude of Christ, one gives oneself to the will of God. Peter said, "He that has suffered in the flesh has ceased from sin" (v. 1). Through suffering in the will of God, Christ dealt with our sins that he might bring us to God. When a person commits herself to Christ in faith to the extent that the will of God is accepted, her life is set upon a principle that is different than the will of the flesh. The person who suffers because she is outside of the will of God will sin in her suffering. The person who is suffering because she is in the will of God will not sin in her suffering, but will praise and worship God. Stephen was stoned to death. It would have been natural for him to fight back and curse his assailants, but he prayed for their forgiveness and worshiped God as he died. He was in the will of God as he suffered, so he did not respond to suffering with sin, but in holiness of life.

This commitment to the will of God is to be made for the rest of life in the flesh. There are many people who depend upon the emotional responses of the moment to supply them with their religious strength. When this is done, sometimes one is strong and sometimes one is weak. Peter said that our commitment to the will of God is to be for the rest of our earthly lives. People ought to take the will of God as the guidelines for life. It is not enough to be revived for today only, but we need to turn all that we are over to God forever.

Verse 4 indicates that commitment to the will of God will be thought strange by the world. This will be discussed more later. Now let me simply say that it is more important to be in the will of God than anything else, even though the world thinks it strange.

The other will to be considered is human will. This will must coincide with the will of God. For this to be done, the human will must be tamed. What is it that is to be tamed? Peter called it the "will of the Gentiles" (v. 3). He was simply saying that there is a desire of life that is common to people outside of God. He described that way of life with five words, which the following paragraphs will discuss.

The way of the human will is characterized by *licentiousness* or excess. The person who does not have his life placed in the hands of God does not have any boundaries. Some people even boast that they do not have anything to "fence them in." Every life must have some limits upon it, or it will destroy itself. Excessive amounts of many things will completely obliterate the meaning of life. The so-called "new morality" concept of life is licentious. Can people really live by taking anything they want in excess? No, a person could even kill himself on excessive amounts of banana pudding.

The second characteristic of the human will is *drunkenness.* The word translated *drunkenness* means to bubble up or overflow. When the will of God is not taken in the human life, people often turn to alcohol or drugs. This offers a temporary reprieve from reality. The trouble is the reprieve is very temporary and very wrong.

The third word that describes the human will means revellings. Peter was saying that the person outside of the will of God lives in a kind of fantasy world. Christians are sometimes accused of living in "ivory towers," but it is really those out of Christ who do. By social revellings, they think that they "buy up" the good of life. The bubble always breaks.

The next word is often translated *carousings.* It means drinking bouts. The human will may sometimes lead to gross abuses of life. Some people become alcoholics or dope addicts as the result of their human wills.

The last characteristic that Peter expressed is *lawless idolatry.* People outside of the will of God will create gods for themselves; but it will not be the real living God, who has revealed himself through Christ. Nearly every person in the world has made her own god. She defends her concept of this god because the little god agrees with her total way of life outside of the will of God. This is the lawless idolatry of the human will.

One cannot be in the will of the world and in the will of God. Peter said that the past time is sufficient for the human will to have reigned in our lives. If we are to have the attitude of victory which Christ had in suffering, then we must turn from the will of the world to the will of God.

The Bad Attitude

A losing attitude is discussed in verses 4-6. The people who are outside of Christ cannot commit themselves to the will of God. They cannot share the attitude of Christ. They are losers. Their losing attitude is seen in the surprise which they have in the commitment of the Christian to God, "in which they are astonished at your not walking with them in wasteful excess" (v. 4). Sin has always wanted company. Eve invited Adam to join her in sin as soon as she had sinned. People seem to enjoy getting others to be part of their sin. This is probably true because people think that there is vindication in social acceptance.

People outside the will of God want to be able to feel that their sinful ways of life are not only acceptable but also they are good. Therefore, they are not only astonished when other people live in the will of God but also are critical. In verse 4, Peter said that these astonished people of the world speak evil of those who do not join them.

The ultimate loss that comes to them is aptly expressed in judgment. Peter said that they may be able to criticize the faithful people of God, but finally, they must render an account to God himself. God is the judge of the living and the dead. He judges now, and he will judge in eternity. He judges the saved and the unsaved. No one at any time can escape the judgment of God. One may not commit himself to the will of God. He may even criticize those who do, but he will be required to render an account to God in this matter.

There is no one who will have any excuse to escape judgment. Verse 6 says, "For this cause also was the gospel proclaimed to the dead, that they might be judged according to God in the Spirit." Many people refer this verse to the previous chapter, saying that it refers to the descent into hell. It seems, however, that Peter was saying the gospel had been preached to people who are dead spiritually so that they might have an opportunity to have spiritual life. If they do not believe the gospel, they have no excuse.

There is an offer in verse 6. The person whose attitude is contrary to the will of Christ will be judged in this losing attitude, but Christ can make that attitude new.

The Best Attitude

Peter next wrote about the elements of the victorious attitude.

But the end of all things has drawn near: therefore exercise self-control and be sober in prayer: before all things having zealous love unto yourselves, because love conceals many sins: showing hospitality to each other without murmuring: just as each received a gift, ministering it unto yourselves as good stewards of the manifold grace of God; if anyone is speaking, let it be as a word from God; if anyone serves, let it be as out of the power which God supplies: that in all things God might be glorified through Jesus Christ, who is the glory and power forever, Amen (vv. 7-11).

Expectation is the first element of the victorious attitude. One of the dominating factors of thought for Christians in the first century was the return of Jesus. Peter was constantly encouraged by his belief that the Lord was about to return to the earth. The first readers of Peter's letter were told that they could take courage in suffering because the end of all things was at hand. Expectation concerning the return of the Lord is one of the most encouraging things that any Christian can have. Today as Christians suffer in sin, they are able to possess that same expectancy. The Lord has promised to return, and he will certainly do it. We cannot know when he will come, but we can know that he will. He has not left the world to run down without hope. He will come to receive his own unto himself.

I recently read a novel about a slave who lived just prior to the Civil War. He could not believe that liberation would ever come, but he kept his hope alive by praying for a "Moses" to appear. In the slavery of sin which brings its anguish to the Christian, we do not lose hope because we know that Jesus is coming again.

When Jesus comes, he will receive his own unto himself in perfect fellowship. No matter how difficult life is now, it will be perfect then. Those who are called upon to suffer are able to endure their suffering because they have hope based upon the expectation of Jesus' return to earth.

Growing out of this expectancy are two qualities of life that will strengthen Christians. Self-control is the first of these. Peter said that people must not let their lives go unbridled. In commitment to God's will, people are to keep their humanity under control at all times by submitting everything that they are to the Lord. The second quality is sobriety. This is realized in prayer. The suffering person could lose sobriety and become a disoriented thinker, but the Lord says that person should remain sober in prayer. Through constant conversation with God, we are able to stay in fellowship with him so that God gives us the element of sobriety as we expect and wait for the Lord's return to the earth.

In verses 8-9 it is evident that love is an element of the victorious attitude. In fact, Peter said that this element is to be held above all things. The love that we exercise toward one another will cover a multitude of sins. Peter did not mean that we can get God to overlook overt acts of sin by loving each other. He meant that our love for each other will keep us from committing sins against each other. The love that Peter was talking about is not just a love that we say we have; we are to show that we have it. He said that love is to be demonstrated by exercising hospitality to each other without murmuring. Hospitality simply means acts of kindness. To be kind toward fellow Christians voluntarily is the demonstration of love. If Christians truly accept the victorious attitude of Christ while living in today's world, this love will be in our lives.

The third element of the victorious attitude is seen in the proper exercise of spiritual gifts. This is, of course, related to the element of love. All of God's people are given spiritual gifts. Each one has different gifts, but they all come from God. Peter said that Christians are to use their gifts as good stewards of the many-sided grace of God. People are not to be jealous of each other in the gifts that they have received, but they are to realize that since these gifts came from God they are to be used for the benefit of all of God's people.

If God gives one the ability to speak, then he is to speak a word from God. He is not to use such a gift for his own benefit but in the will of God. This means that the gift will become beneficial to all who hear him speak and to God as well.

If God gives a person the gift of ministering, she is not to do it in her own strength or ability but by the power which God supplies. Too many ministries of the church today are done out of human ability, and too few are done out of the power which God supplies. This is true because people have not let the victorious attitude of Christ be theirs in commitment to the perfect will of God.

People have been eager to get glory for themselves in the ministry of the gifts that God has placed at their disposal. Peter said that God ought to be glorified in all things through Christ. In seeking glory for ourselves, we lose the power of God and become failures. When we serve in the glory of Christ, the power of God succeeds.

Peter said that we are to serve each other with our gifts by giving ourselves completely to Christ in everything that we do. Christ, then, will gain the victory. We may be short on ability, but Christ never fails.

Life will have its hardships. God has never promised to remove trials and suffering. But we can have victory in hardships and sufferings if our attitude is right.

The soldier who wins a victory must have the right equipment, and the Christian who wins the victory must have the right equipment also. The right equipment for the battle of suffering is to be *armed with the attitude of Christ: submission to the will of God.*

12
In the Fiery Furnace

1 Peter 4:12-19

The Book of Daniel has many fascinating stories about God's care for his people when they are tried. One of the most interesting of these stories is found in Daniel 3. The Babylonian king, Nebuchadnezzar, had made a golden image, which he expected everyone to worship. Shadrach, Meshach, and Abednego, who were faithful to Jehovah, refused to worship the image. When this was reported to Nebuchadnezzar, he became very angry and sentenced them to be put to death by the flames of a fiery furnace.

The Bible is very dramatic in its description of the intense heat of the furnace. However, the heat could not destroy these three faithful men. The Word of God says that they were called out of the flames unharmed without even the smell of smoke on their clothing. While they were in the fiery furnace, Nebuchadnezzar saw not three but four people in the flames. He described the appearance of the fourth as being like the Son of God. It is quite clear that the Scripture is saying that God took care of his faithful people in their time of fiery trial.

Peter said that God will always take care of his people in fiery trials. The fiery trial of today may not be a literal furnace, but it will be a very real trial. In verse 12, Peter said, "Beloved, be not surprised among yourselves at the fiery trial which becomes to you a trial of fidelity, as a strange thing having happened to you." The word which we have translated "fiery" indicates that the trial is a testing period. Earlier Peter had mentioned that faith is tried by the fire of suffering, like gold refined by fire. This is an expression of the same idea. Faith must be tried by the fire of suffering. There is a sense in which Christians are cast in the fiery furnace almost daily. They must know how to cope with these trials of faith.

Many people have been cast into the fiery furnace of suffering and have been almost devoured by these flames, but they have come out with a great witness for God. Augustus M. Toplady, who wrote the words to the great hymn "Rock of Ages," spent most of his life in suffering. He developed tuberculosis while he was a college student, and his life was completely wasted by the time he was thirty-eight years old. In his trial, he made a lasting contribution to the spiritual life of succeeding generations.

Charlotte Elliott, who wrote "Just As I Am," lived her entire life in almost unbearable pain. Fanny Crosby, who wrote many of the hymns which we sing, was blind. Rather than being defeated in their fiery furnaces these people walked with God.

Through the ages, many Christians have been cast by the world into the fiery furnace, but one in appearance like the Son of God has walked beside them. Peter knew much about walking in the fiery furnace. Matthew 14 says that Peter attempted to meet Jesus while Jesus was walking on the water. Peter began his journey toward Christ on the water wonderfully well, but as he saw what he was doing, he began to sink. His faith was being tried. The loving hand of the Master reached out to lift him from his fear. The early chapters of Acts record that Peter was on several occasions arrested. Once he was ordered by the Sanhedrin to stop preaching but Peter went away rejoicing that he could walk in the fiery furnace with Jesus. On another occasion, he was placed in a maximum security cell. The Lord came and brought him out so that he could continue the ministry to which he had been called. Surely God was with Peter in the fiery furnace.

Will you and I ever be cast into the fiery furnace? We won't be cast into Nebuchadnezzar's furnace, most likely we will never be arrested because we are Christians. Nor are our trials the same as those faced by the Christians to whom Peter wrote his epistle. But our faith is tried every day. Satan is no different now than he was in the first century. He wants us to fail when the time of testing comes. In 1 Peter 4:12-19, there is instruction that will help us face the trial by fire that must be faced today.

Composed

In facing the fiery trials that are with us today, we must learn to be composed. Peter stated it negatively by saying, "Be not surprised among yourselves at the fiery trials." Many of the people who first received his letter were probably Gentile Christians. The Jews were accustomed to persecution but these Gentiles were probably not accustomed to any kind of persecution for religious reasons. Peter was saying that they should not be surprised when such persecution comes. He said, "Do not look upon it as though a strange thing has happened to you" (v. 12). Many people today have great difficulty in obeying this command. Most people think something strange has happened whenever things go wrong for them.

As a pastor I have heard such remarks as this, "I just can't understand why God let something like this happen to me." Such a comment means: "Since I am a Christian and serving the Lord, it is a strange thing that I have any reversals in life." On the contrary, Peter said it is not a strange thing. Rather than going to pieces when the chips are down, we should be composed. It is a natural thing that one who belongs to the Lord would suffer. This suffering is a refiner. Just as a piece of steel gains character in the fire, so the life of a Christian becomes the life of strength and fervent character because it is refined in the fire of suffering.

Peter actually suggested that we rejoice in our suffering. This seems to be a very strange command. Can one really rejoice while in pain or mental anguish? Certainly we would not rejoice over pain, nor would we rejoice over the mental anguish. But some great benefits are brought to us as we walk through the fiery furnace of suffering. The Christian is able to rejoice because of these benefits. Peter said that one of the great benefits of suffering is fellowship with the sufferings of Christ.

In Matthew 16:24 Jesus said, "If any man will come after me, let him deny himself, and take up his cross, and follow me" (KJV). Jesus was saying that his disciples should expect to bear a cross. It is only a natural thing that we should participate in the suffering of Christ as well as in the glory of Christ. Jesus also said,

If the world hate you, ye know that it hated me before it hated you. If ye were of the world, the world would love his own: but because ye are not of the world, but I have chosen you out of the world, therefore the world hateth you. Remember the word that I said unto you, The servant is not greater than his lord. If they have persecuted me, they will also persecute you; if they have kept my saying, they will keep yours also (John 15:18-20 KJV).

Paul said that he was a partaker of the suffering of Christ because the crucified Christ was his new life. Certainly it is not pleasant to suffer. However, when we realize that we are sharing in the suffering of Jesus, who suffered that we might be redeemed from the guilt of sin, there is cause to rejoice in our suffering. Knowing that we are having fellowship with him in suffering, we know also that he is bearing us up and giving up his strength. The most joyous thing about life in this world is to walk with Jesus, even if we are walking with him in suffering.

Peter said that this fellowship with Christ in suffering has a great promise for the future. He said that we will have reason to rejoice in the revelation of Christ's glory. It will be rejoicing with great joy. The Christians of the first century were called upon to suffer death, but Peter wanted them to be reminded that, when Jesus comes again to reveal the glory of the Father unto them, there would be no more suffering but only rejoicing. Surely we can rejoice in any pain, in any discomfort, in any mental or emotional anxiety while here upon the earth if we remember that the suffering is in fellowship with Jesus Christ for the glory of God. Ultimately we will be rewarded by the wonderful presence of Jesus himself.

A third command concerns the composure we ought to have in our fiery furnace. Peter said, "Be happy even if you are reviled in the name of Jesus, because the spirit of glory and the spirit of God rests upon you to actuate you" (v. 14). This very acutely reminds us of the words of Jesus in Matthew 5:10-11, "Blessed are they which are persecuted for righteousness' sake: for theirs is the kingdom of heaven. Blessed are ye, when men shall revile you, and persecute you, and shall say all manner of evil against you falsely, for my sake" (KJV).

The word which is translated *revile* in verse 14 refers to more than the occasional revilings by certain hostile individuals. It refers to the fury of an entire mob who would stand against the child of God. It seems very strange to tell one to be happy when there is mob violence against one, but Peter was instructing first-century Christians, and God is instructing us, to be happy under these circumstances.

It is very difficult to understand a part of verse 14. Though we cannot fully understand what Peter meant when he said, "The spirit of glory and the spirit of God rests upon you," we can know that it is a glorious promise. We can be happy even while we walk through the fiery furnace of crowd disapproval because we have the approval of God. In this approval, God will glorify us inwardly by the working of his Holy Spirit. We do not need the approval of the crowds to be what we really ought to be in the sight of God.

Organized Christianity today spends more energy than is necessary trying to find the world's approval. Christians must have better guidelines than these which say that we are to have everyone's approval. It is important that we have the approval of God. When the Spirit of God's glory rests upon us, then we can continually rejoice, even if we stand alone. People who have been burned at the stake have rejoiced as they died because they died in the glory of the Spirit of God.

Peter said that the Spirit of God resting upon us will actually empower us. The word which is translated *rests* is a word which literally means "to rest upon one, to actuate that person." The Lord empowers through the Holy Spirit, making it possible for us to have whatever strength is needed when we walk through a fiery furnace of reviling. We may not know how to endure the suffering that must be endured, but if we trust the Lord, he gives us the strength.

Let us not lose our composure when we face the fiery furnace of life, but let us accept it as a thing that must be and should be instead of some strange thing. Let us also remember that we are having fellowship with Christ in a very unusual sense when we suffer. Therefore, let us be happy and wait upon the Spirit of God to give to us the strength that is necessary to walk in the fiery furnace.

Christian

In verses 15-18 there is a command to suffer as a Christian. Peter began with a negative statement, "For let none of you suffer as a murderer or a thief, or as an evildoer, or as a meddler in men's affairs" (v. 15). Many people think that they are walking in the fiery furnace when they suffer because they have done things that are wrong. I remember reading in a local newspaper about a politician who had been caught in a very ugly sin. The next day he made the statement that he knew how Christ felt when he was crucified. Christ was not crucified for doing wrong, but he was crucified because others did wrong.

We are not to think of ourselves as having fellowship in the suffering of Christ when we suffer because of our sins. We are not walking in the fiery furnace when we suffer as a murderer, a thief, an evildoer, or as a meddler in other's affairs. Much suffering in the world today can be explained as the natural consequences of the deeds of people. If we bring such suffering on ourselves, we do not need to expect the intervention of God.

In verse 16 Peter said, "But if a man suffers as a Christian let him be unashamed, but let him glorify God in this name." A Christian is one who is like Jesus. The word *Christian* is not often used in the New Testament. Both here and in the Book of Acts, it is a name that is applied to those who follow Jesus by those who do not follow Jesus. In the first century Christians expected to suffer for their beliefs. In the twentieth century, Christians who live as they should must also expect suffering. There are certain sacrifices that will become absolutely necessary if we live as Christians. However, Peter said that one should not be ashamed. Christians should glorify God in the name of Christ which they bear.

Recently a young Christian called me, asking my opinion about some questionable conduct in which he wished to engage. After I expressed my opinion, he said that to really live for Jesus was going to be most embarrassing for him because his friends would not understand. The Lord said we should be unashamed, even though our friends do not understand. Rather than being ashamed of the name Christian, one should glory that the name of Christ can be applied to one's life.

The reason for this is expressed in verses 17-18. Peter said, "Because the time for judgment to begin from the house of God has come; but if it begins first from us; what is the end of the ones not persuaded by the gospel of God, and if the just is barely saved where shall the ungodly and sinner appear?" In suffering, judgment does begin from the house of God. Someone might say, "If the Christian has to walk through the fiery furnace, would it not be better if I were not a Christian in today's world?"

Peter said it would be far worse if you were not a Christian. Christians walk through the refiners' fire, but those who are not persuaded by the gospel of God to be Christians are not saved at all. They must face a far greater judgment than Christians face as they go through the fiery furnace of life.

Committed

The third instruction for us, as we walk through the fiery furnace, is to be committed. In verse 19 Peter said, "Wherefore also, the ones who are suffering according to the will of God, let them commit their souls in well doing to the faithful creator." The suffering that we experience when we walk through the fiery furnace is suffering in the will of God. God permitted the three Hebrews to be cast into the fiery furnace in order that his name might be glorified. God permits us also to endure hardships in this life in order that his name might be glorified in the refining of our faith. For his name to be glorified to the maximum, we must commit our souls unto him. There is no other way for us to endure the flames of suffering. Many people do not endure, though they claim to be Christians. There are many church members who have fallen by the wayside. There are many people who have taught in Sunday School classes and faithfully attended church for years, yet have fallen when the time of suffering came. Jesus said that there would be people like this.

In the parable of the sower, Jesus said that there were some of the seeds that fell on the stony ground. Their roots were not very strong, therefore, when the sun of persecution came up they withered and died. If we do not commit ourselves in faith to the faithful Creator, our lives will collapse in the time of suffering. But if we do commit ourselves to this faithful Creator, he will make it possible for us to live for him even while we suffer. God gives the victory in suffering.

We can argue about suffering. We can seek to explain suffering. We can read volumes on suffering, but there is one answer to our personal needs in suffering. That answer is to commit our souls to God. When we do this, he will come in to reign in our lives. He will be our victory over suffering. Whatever form this suffering might take, he will be our victory. If we have revilings from the people about us, he will be our victory, but he cannot be our victory unless we commit all that we are to him.

This passage of Scripture explains trials more than does any other passage in the Bible. We need to remember the three commands that God has placed before us. He has told us to be *composed,* to be *Christian,* and to be *committed.*

Whatever trial comes to you, if you will approach that trial composed by accepting the trial as a usual thing in fellowship with the Lord Jesus Christ, and rejoicing as you accept it, you will have a new courage. If you will accept your trial as a Christian without shame, glorifying God because he has redeemed you from trial in the world to come, you will have a new hope. If you will accept your trial by committing yourself unto the power of God, you will have a complete victory.

13
Standing in the Grace of God

1 Peter 5:1-14

The conclusion to the book of 1 Peter expresses the heart of the entire message. In verse 12 Peter said that he wrote, "Encouraging and testifying that this is the true grace of God." He told the readers to stand fast in this true grace of God. There is no better place to be when trouble comes than in the very center of the grace of God.

People have sought to find an answer to their needs almost everywhere except the grace of God. Some people have thought that the answer to their needs could be found in gaining greater wealth, but greater wealth brought no satisfaction. Some have thought that security came to life with the gaining of political power or some other power over other people. This also has failed in the time of need. Like Samson, many great people have fallen when they depended upon their own strength.

The readers of 1 Peter needed the grace of God more than anything else. It has already been evident to us that these people were in great suffering, and nothing could give them the strength that was necessary for their lives except the grace of God. In verse 10 Peter said, "And the God of all grace, who called you unto his eternal glory in Christ, after that ye have suffered a little while, shall himself perfect, establish, and strengthen you." When one is called unto the eternal glory of Christ by grace, he may suffer for a little while, but God has some better things for him. God will be with him to give grace while he is suffering. The instruction that God has for those who suffer now is that they should stand in the grace of God while they are suffering.

Grace for Shepherds

The first four verses of chapter 5 say that the grace of God is sufficient for Christian leaders. This paragraph is addressed particularly to ministers. Peter said, "Therefore I beseech the elders among you, who am a fellow elder and witness of the sufferings of Christ, who am also a fellow sharer of the coming glory" (v. 1). The term *elder* simply means an older person. But it is commonly believed that the word had an official meaning. Peter thought that he had a right to address such a group as this because he also was an elder. More than this, he was a "witness of the sufferings of Christ." This probably means that he saw the sufferings of Christ and that he had had the privilege of sharing in the suffering of Christ throughout his life. He also believed that he would be a sharer in the glory of Christ when he returned to the earth.

Peter told the elders that God's assignment to them is to shepherd the flock of God. They were not to give up because they lived in a time of suffering. The flock of God must be tended. Today there are many ministers who are giving up because of difficulties. Almost every week news comes of a fellow minister who has left his assignment because he is disillusioned with the ministry of the church. If God's minister expects his life to be easy and victorious, in the sense that the world counts victorious, he will give up. God's minister must expect that there will be times of difficulty and suffering, but the flock must be tended.

Sometimes God's flock is in great difficulty. There are times when God assigns his minister to a flock that is torn by strife, financial difficulties, or other problems. We cannot measure the call of God by the attractiveness of the congregation. There are poor, downtrodden flocks, but they are still the flock of God. There are small rural churches almost unknown, but they are the flock of God. The flock must be tended. The post must not be left. God's shepherd must accept his assignment.

Peter said that the assignment to shepherd the flock is not to be accepted by force but willingly. He meant by this that the shepherd is not to be forced by any external thing, but he is to do his task because it is the will of God. The shepherd is not to tend the flock for any personal reason but because God wants him to do it. He is not to shepherd the flock for any base gain for himself. The words which are translated "filthy lucre" (v. 2) mean more than money. They mean eagerness for base gain. The minister is not to serve for any reason of personal gain, whether it be fame, a pat on the back, or success. Ministers are simply to serve because they feel called of God to do so and because God has given them flocks to tend.

The principle in these verses can be applied to all Christian leaders. It is not just for pastors, but anyone who serves the Lord ought to serve willingly. Many people in the church today serve because they are constrained to do so. This makes for unsuccessful service. God will give grace to his shepherd who tends the flock because it is God's will for him to do so. He will also give grace to any Christian leader who serves simply because it is God's will. The context of this passage is teaching that the Christian must serve even in hard times with an eager, willing spirit. When one does, God will give grace to be successful.

Verse 3 teaches us that the shepherd is to use grace properly. Peter simply said that the elder is not to serve, "as lording it over the allotment but by becoming an example to the flock." The motivation for service is important, but the way one serves is also important. Rather than trying to lead people by telling them what they must do, the worker in God's kingdom shows by example the way of life in God's grace.

The fullness of God's grace for the Christian servant who serves even under stress will be understood when Jesus returns. In verse 4 Peter said, "When the chief Shepherd is manifested, you will obtain the unfading crown of glory" (RSV). The shepherd, who tends his flock and suffers because he does so; or the Christian teacher, who teaches a class and suffers in doing so, can be sure that there is a time of reward for faithful service. The crowns of glory that shall come to faithful servants are unfading crowns. The Christian servant may cast her eyes upon the glory of that crown now while she suffers, and the beautiful illuminating vision will not fade out. The chief Shepherd, who is Jesus, will bring the crown of glory with him for all who have served him faithfully through times of suffering.

This was great comfort to first-century Christians. Even if they lost their lives for the sake of Jesus, there would be great glory for them in his presence in eternity. That is still true today. It is worth all the suffering and all the disappointments that are endured now to receive the unfading crown of glory from the chief Shepherd when he comes.

Grace for Sheep

Verses 5-9 teach that there is sufficient grace for all of the followers of Christ. God gives grace to those who are humble enough to follow the leadership of the Shepherd. Peter said, "Likewise, young men, be obedient to the elders, and let all gird yourselves in humility, because God resists the haughty but gives grace to the humble ones" (v. 5). The grace of God is sufficient for all who would follow Jesus in humility.

Peter said that the followers were to gird themselves in humility. The word which is translated "gird" is a word which was used to describe an apron which slaves wore. This apron was fastened to the girdle of the vest and distinguished slaves from free men. It's use in this verse means to gird oneself with humility as the servant of Christ. By putting on humility, one shows his subjection to another, just as the slave showed his subjection to his master by putting on the apron of slavery.

This passage says three things about humility. First, humility is a necessary spirit in order to serve one another. The grace of God is available for this service of humility. God did not intend for Christians to live for themselves but that our lives would be used to influence other people. Only in humility can this be done.

In verse 6 Peter said, "Therefore let us humble ourselves under the strong hand of God in order that he might exalt you in due time." This verse expresses the second reason for humility as being the ultimate exaltation of the humble. God demands that people humble themselves under his strong hand in order that his grace might be operative in their lives. This humility is to be expressed to one another, and it is to be done in the will of God. Christians do not have the right to do as they please, only the right to do as God pleases.

If such humility is demonstrated, God will exalt the Christian. The word that is translated *exalt* is a word which means to lift up in exaltation. This same word is used to refer to the cross in John 3:14. Christ was lifted up in suffering on the cross but his suffering was his victory. In humbling ourselves before God to do his will, we may be asked to suffer, but the very act of suffering will become our exaltation or victory because God will give us grace.

The third reason for humility is expressed in verse 7. Peter instructed his readers to cast all of their anxieties upon God because God cares about them. Christians may have cares or anxieties as they suffer in the service of God, but they must not forget that God cares. We are to throw our anxieties upon him, and he will take care of them. The word which is translated "care" means to be drawn in different directions. Life is always drawing us in different directions. This causes anxiety. God can take care of all of these anxieties because he draws in one direction.

Followers receive grace when they express their humility, but it is also found in the expression of sobriety of life. Peter said, "Be sober, be watchful your adversary the devil as a roaring lion walks about seeking whom to devour" (v. 8). God gives his grace to people who are sober and watchful enough to realize that the devil can beset their lives.

There is no immunity from the temptations of the devil. Like a roaring lion, he never gives up but walks about seeking to devour the influence of every Christian life if possible. Peter said that the Christian should withstand the devil. This is done by being firm in the faith. Especially in the time of suffering, the devil tries to devour the Christian. The devil says it is not worth all of the suffering to work for God or to be in God's will. It would be very easy to believe him. In fact, many people do believe him. But God will give grace to those who are sober and watchful and those who are steadfast in the faith.

There is not enough human strength to stand against the devil, but when God is added to the human life, the Christian has enough strength to stand against the devil. God's grace fills our hearts and renders the devil helpless when we are committed completely to him. God's grace for all followers is sufficient when they are watchful in sobriety, submitted to the Lord. The devil cannot win victory over people committed to God.

Verse 10 expresses the strength of God's grace. "The God who called you unto his eternal glory in Christ after suffering a little shall make you what you ought to be, shall confirm your mind, shall make you strong, shall found you." Peter's God is the God of all grace. There are absolutely no limitations upon this grace. The God of all grace, of unlimited power, of unlimited fellowship with believers, of unlimited concern, care, and mercy calls his children unto his eternal glory in Christ.

Before the fullness of this glory is revealed, there is a little suffering. The suffering is small when compared to the fullness of the eternal glory in Christ, but while God's children are going through "a little while" (RSV) of suffering, God gives grace. This grace makes God's children what they ought to be. The word which is translated "strengthen" means to bring one back into the right way by correction. To do this makes a person what he ought to be. It may take suffering for a person to be brought back into the right way, but by grace God will give to the person this strength even in suffering.

God does more than make us what we ought to be, he confirms our minds in the fact that he is working in our lives. This means that even while the Christian is suffering, God is saying, "I am with you; I am your strength; I will not fail you; you are confirmed in me." Peter added that God makes his children strong and lays a foundation for their lives. The God of all grace gives exactly what each person needs when they are trusting in him. Suffering is a little thing when it is compared to the power of God. It is no wonder that Peter would conclude his marvelous epistle by saying, "To God be power forever" (v. 11).

Looking back through the entire epistle, a note of victory has been sounded in every verse. Though the readers were called strangers, God had elected them, and this was victory. Peter had taught them that victory was always possible to those who pulled themselves together with faith and holiness.

Because of the victory that God has for suffering Christians, they were to put off all the things that were foreign to God and surrender themselves totally to God's victorious way of life. In this kind of surrender, one could endure every injustice. Even home life was to be surrendered to God, so that God could make all of life a lovely and beautiful thing. God fills the hearts of the sufferers with a song as they go through life, giving them a victorious salvation that is full and complete.

The world today counts suffering as defeat, but it is not a defeat for Christians. Faith must be tried by fire, but when the object of faith is Jesus Christ, the result is victory. The grace of God will stand every test. "Stand ye fast therein" (v. 12).

Bibliography

Beare, Francis W. *The First Epistle of Peter.* Oxford: Blackwell, 1947. (This commentary seeks to reconstruct the Greek text and to disprove Petrine authorship. It has a good discussion of the theology of the epistle.)

Bigg, Charles. *A Critical and Exegetical Commentary on the Epistles of St. Peter and St. Jude.* Edinburgh: T. & T. Clark, 1956. (This commentary from the International Critical series is an excellent exegesis.)

Cranfield, C.E.B. *The First Epistle of Peter.* London: S.C.M. Press, 1954. (A brief work combining exegesis and exposition.)

Hort, F.J.A. *The First Epistle of Peter 1:1-11:17.* London: Macmillan and Co., 1898. Reprinted by James & Clock Publishing Co., Minneapolis, Mn., 1976. (This work was written posthumously from Hort's notes. It is very good, but limited to introductory matters and comments on a brief part of First Peter.)

Lenski, R.C.H. *The Interpretation of the Epistle of St. Peter, St. John and St. Jude.* Minneapolis: Augsburg Publishing House, 1966. (There is a concise statement in this work of the introductory matters. The Greek text is explained for an English reader.)

Meyer, F.B. *Tried by Fire.* Grand Rapids: Baker Book House, 1950. (A nice, brief exposition of First Peter.)

Selwyn, Edward G. *The First Epistle of St. Peter.* London: Macmillan & Co., 1952. (A classical work with many additional notes. One of the most important publications on 1 Peter.)

Summers, Ray. *1 Peter,* The Broadman Bible Commentary, Vol. 12. Nashville: Broadman Press, 1972. (A very good commentary written in a very readable way. A very practical approach is made to introductory matters.)